RENEWAL

a journal of social democracy

Vol 21 No. 1

Renewal welcomes contributions

We will consider articles from anyone involved with the process of politics and ideas. These can be in the form of new articles and essays, or 'feedback' pieces on existing published articles. We also welcome suggestions for articles and potential authors. To submit or discuss articles please email editorial@renewal.org.uk

Published by **Renewal Limited**
www.renewal.org.uk
in association with
Lawrence & Wishart
99a Wallis Road
London E9 5LN

Follow Renewal on Twitter: @RENEWALjournal
Like Renewal on Facebook: https://www.facebook.com/Renewal.journal.of.social.democracy

ISSN 0968-252X
ISBN 978-1-907103-75-9

Designed by Fran Davies
Typeset by e-type, Liverpool
Printed in Devon by ImprintDigital

RENEWAL Vol 21 No. 1

Editorial policy statement

Renewal is a quarterly journal of politics and ideas, committed to exploring and expanding the progressive potential of social democracy.

Social democracy has always been a complex and contested political tradition. *Renewal* offers a space in which the historic purposes of social democracy – the expansion of equality, democratic governance, and social freedoms – can be debated, advanced, and applied to contemporary politics. The last three decades, lived under the shadow of neo-liberalism, have been testing ones for advocates of these objectives. But there are reasons to think that the politics of the next three decades can be different. Financial crisis, recession, and austerity have thrown into sharp relief the instability, unfairness, and cynicism of the neo-liberal era. Social democratic solutions, drawing on ancestral commitments to market regulation, social partnership, and the egalitarian sharing of benefits and burdens, are gaining greater purchase in public debate. But it will require careful thought and a bruising political struggle to move these commitments from oppositional discourse into a coherent and powerful political project capable of commanding public support and ultimately building a good society.

Renewal aims to provide a forum in which such a revitalised social democratic prospectus can be formulated and debated. To do so, it will span the realms of social action, academic research, political activism, and policy development. It will develop a critical analysis of existing conditions and current trends, but will also seek to uncover and connect to countervailing forces, emerging alternatives, and new sites of progressive agency. *Renewal* will explore what social democracy can learn from other allied political traditions, and how the insights of movements such as feminism, environmentalism, and social liberalism challenge and modify social democratic politics.

Renewal will remain closely engaged with the future of British politics but will also seek to broaden its vision, making sense of global changes, analysing developments in social democracy outside of Britain, and making links with international movements. A particular concern will be to contribute to the project of designing a co-ordinated alternative which social democracy can advance in its historic European heartland.

Renewal aims to subject the left's politics to honest, constructive, and rigorous scrutiny, since such fundamental discussion is an integral component of the creation of any successful left-wing political project. *Renewal* therefore offers serious debate, encouraging a productive confrontation of different perspectives and programmes by airing their arguments in their strongest form.

Above all, *Renewal* will continue to offer a focus and a gathering point for the ideas and analysis necessary to the formulation of a viable and radical political strategy for a twenty-first century left. We invite support, and encourage contributions, from all who share that objective.

Guest editorial

Can One Nation Labour learn from the British New Left?

Madeleine Davis

The early British New Left – a vibrant activist and intellectual current that flourished between 1956 and 1963 and whose brief lifespan encompassed the early careers of many of the most important British socialist intellectuals of the last half-century – has made an unexpected recent return to the political stage. In the ongoing discussion about ideological renewal within the British Labour Party, figures associated with the 'Blue' and latterly 'One Nation' Labour tendencies, particularly Jon Cruddas and his collaborator Jonathan Rutherford, have cited the ideas of prominent New Leftists, most often Edward Thompson and Raymond Williams, in support of their arguments for a politics that seeks to re-connect Labour traditions to English culture and society (Cruddas and Rutherford, 2010; Rutherford, 2011).

On 27 June 2012, a conference in Westminster brought representatives of these two currents together. With contributions from historians of the New Left and of Labour, as well as figures involved in policy-making or implementation, the conference explored common-alities and differences and posed the question: what, if anything, is of value in an engagement between these two intellectual traditions? This special issue reproduces revised versions of three of the contributions made to that conference, those by Jonathan Rutherford, labour movement historian Mark Wickham-Jones, and longstanding activist and intellectual of the New Left and founder-editor of *Soundings*, Michael Rustin. It also includes a fourth piece solicited subsequently from Michael Kenny, author of the key study of the early New Left's political thought, and currently working on a major study of the politics of English nationhood (Kenny, 1995). All would wish to acknowledge with gratitude the contributions to the day's discussion of a distinguished line-up of speakers, including Hilary Wainwright, Anthony Barnett, Maurice Glasman, Michael Walzer, Robin Archer, Nick Stevenson, Paul Nowak, Tess Lanning, Marc Stears and Jon Cruddas.

The New Left as a source for Labour's ideological renewal

At first sight the New Left may appear an unlikely source from which to draw inspiration for contemporary debates within Labour. 'A plague o' both your houses' described its attitude to the twin 'declining orthodoxies' of Stalinism and social democracy, and it produced some of the sharpest and best-known critiques of the Labour Party and its role in British politics. For the most part it viewed 'Labourism' (a term denoting the structural subordination of Labour within the British state and constitutional order) as a positive obstacle to the development of the authentically socialist politics it sought to foster

(Miliband, 1961; Nairn, 1964a, b and c; Davis, 2003). Yet in none of its manifestations did it offer any lasting or definite resolution to the strategic and organisational dilemma that this conviction posed, and in its own – rather intermittent – political practice the New Left repeatedly faltered over the question of whether to sponsor any initiative in direct competition with Labour, even when most convinced of the necessity to do so.

Critics of the New Left's political incapacity have sometimes presented this as intellectual dilettantism, or a refusal to put principle to the test of reality, but it is more accurately grasped as a genuine and deep ambivalence. For the question of its relationship to the Labour Party bedevilled the New Left from its inception in 1956, when resignees from the British Communist Party, notably Marxist historians Edward Thompson and John Saville, formed the earliest of the milieu's key journals, *The New Reasoner*. Joining forces with a younger group of independent socialists that included Stuart Hall, then a doctoral student at Oxford; philosopher Charles Taylor; and energetic student radical Raphael (Ralph) Samuel, who had established *Universities and Left Review* in 1957, the two journals merged as *New Left Review* (*NLR*) in 1960, picking up Ralph Miliband and Raymond Williams – two key figures not fitting neatly into either group – along the way. From 'parallelism' – the 'one foot in, one foot out' position adopted by the early New Left circa 1959 as they sought to challenge the influence of Croslandite revisionism within the party – through to the critical support offered in the early 1980s to Bennism, and even notwithstanding the 'let it bleed' approach to Labour of the *NLR* in its most *Trotskisant* phase, the New Left never resolved this conundrum and – arguably – never entirely gave up on its early efforts to influence the party from the left.

The Labour Party, of course, paid far less attention to the New Left than the New Left paid to it; nor has the New Left critique of Labour attracted much serious attention from historians of the Labour Party (1). To see Jon Cruddas acknowledge the importance for Labour of its encounters with critical traditions 'half in, half out' of the party, therefore, as he did at the final plenary of last year's conference, is surely welcome. Yet doubts remain. Can such an encounter move beyond an opportunistic and selective appropriation to provide a meaningful engagement?

The first – and highly complementary – pair of papers in this collection go to the heart of this issue. Jonathan Rutherford gives a suggestive evocation of the New Left, its project, achievements and limitations that draws some direct comparisons with 'Blue Labour'. Drawing on Jed Esty's reinterpretation of English cultural modernism (2003), Rutherford contends that both these traditions represent an 'effort to frame a specifically English modernity rooted in the radical and conservative traditions of common life'. What he emphasises as of most value in the 'first' New Left – he is far more dismissive of the 'second' *NLR* which eschewed all 'parochialism' and looked instead to continental Marxism – is the 'culture and society' tradition of Raymond Williams, and Edward Thompson's humanist insistence on the importance of the moral imagination. It is this 'English modernity of virtue, humanism and democratic culture', and the New Left's incomplete reworking of the English cultural inheritance, to which 'Blue Labour' is seen as heir.

Esty, however, arguably overplays the congruity between the New Left's oppositional stance and more conservative manifestations of literary and cultural modernism such as those of Leavis and Eliot. It is also worth reminding ourselves just how controversial these issues were within the early New Left itself. Williams' idea of a 'common culture', or of culture as a 'whole way of life', was sharply criticised by Thompson precisely as not doing enough to transcend Eliot's conservative and complacent evocation of English traditions. Culture, Thompson reminded him (and it was a criticism Williams broadly accepted) was a 'whole way of struggle', and the struggle was between class-situated agents (Williams,

1958 and 1961; Thompson, 1961). This is a theme developed by Michael Kenny in the second piece presented here. In a nuanced consideration of the possibilities and implications of the 'progressive patriotism' of Thompson, Kenny reminds us that 'reclaiming English culture and customs for a progressive kind of politics ... involved [for Thompson] the combined exercise of countless individual wills and imaginations, and implied a willingness by radicals to tackle the inequalities of power, wealth and status which were fortified by conservative accounts of the nation'. Though concluding that today's 'progressive patriots' around 'One Nation Labour' should indeed draw inspiration from Thompson, Kenny suggests the latter would – just as he warned Williams – again counsel against 'too great an accommodation with political forms of conservatism'.

The second pair of papers focuses on aspects of the New Left's project that have to date received far less attention than those discussed by Rutherford and Kenny, but which are no less relevant to an assessment of the New Left's contemporary significance and its relationship to Labour traditions. Challenging a prevalent view that sees the New Left as having little to offer by way of an alternative to Croslandite revisionism, Mark Wickham-Jones reappraises one of the most neglected aspects of the early New Left's work – its economic analysis. While conceding that the New Left produced no single volume to rival Crosland's *The Future of Socialism* (1956), he nevertheless contends that the challenge to the revisionist prospectus it made through a series of pieces in early journals and wider left publications was consistent and serious. New Left thinkers refuted the hypotheses of a 'managerial revolution' and of the 'separation of ownership and control' that underpinned Crosland's framework. They advanced new arguments for common ownership, advocating the extension of industrial democracy as a corrective and alternative to the bureaucratic Morrisonian model. They developed proposals for reform of union practices and even a detailed 'Socialist Wages Plan'. Wickham-Jones' analysis provides evidence for the contention that the New Left did indeed present an alternative direction for a reorientation of socialism to rival Crosland's, even if not in the form of an 'overall connected analysis'.

A New Left intervention that precisely set out to provide an 'overall connected analysis' is the subject of the final piece of the four, by Michael Rustin. The product of a recombination of members of the early New Left motivated by their deep disappointment in the Wilson government, the May Day Manifesto Movement of 1967-9 (Thompson, Williams and Hall were key figures along with a younger group that included Rustin himself) attempted to present a coherent 'socialist alternative' to the policies pursued by Labour in government, and a challenge to what was seen as its regressive, superficial and technocratic 'modernisation' (Williams, 1968) (2). If the explicitly socialist frame of reference reminds us how far the terms of debate have shifted, Rustin nevertheless sees contemporary relevance in the New Left's characteristic rejection of the 'willed separation of issues' (on which capitalism depended and in which Labour acquiesced) in favour of an analysis of system crises or, in Gramscian terms, 'conjunctures'. Indeed it is with the aim of sponsoring 'a broader thinking and mapping process ... to influence and inform the current political process' that a new *Soundings* Manifesto has recently been launched, alongside a republication of the original May Day Manifesto.

What shines out of the discussion offered by these four rich papers is the quality and range of the New Left's work. Though of course not without its failures, contradictions, and limitations, it remains one of the most creative intellectual and political currents the British left has produced. A reappraisal by figures within Labour of this often neglected contribution is therefore welcome. Thinkers of 'One Nation Labour' are right to sense the enduring value of the New Left's attempt to root a revitalised left project in contemporary English culture and society, and right too to see in the democratic, humanist and communitarian emphases of the early New Left a valuable 'road not taken', worth renewed exploration. Yet it may also be, as Geoff Andrews (1999) warned in a similar moment of encounter between the New Left and New Labour some years ago, that a search for similarities is rather less useful than retaining the legacy of the New Left as a source of critique.

Madeleine Davis is Lecturer in Politics at Queen Mary, University of London.

References

Andrews, G. (1999) 'New Left and New Labour: modernisation or a new modernity?' *Soundings* 13: 14-24.

Crosland, C. A. R. (1956) *The Future of Socialism*, London, Jonathan Cape.

Cruddas, J. and Rutherford, J. (2010) 'Ethical socialism', *Soundings* 44: 10-21.

Davis, M. (2003) '"Labourism" and the New Left', in Callaghan, J., Fielding, S. and Ludlam, S. (eds.) *Interpreting the Labour Party*, Manchester, Manchester University Press.

Esty, J. (2003) *A Shrinking Island: Modernism and National Culture in England*, Princeton, Princeton University Press.

Foote, G. (1985) *The Labour Party's Political Thought: A History*, Basingstoke, Macmillan.

Jackson, B. (2007) *Equality and the British Left*, Manchester, Manchester University Press.

Kenny, M. (1995) *The First New Left: British Intellectuals after Stalin*, London, Lawrence and Wishart.

Miliband, R. (1961) *Parliamentary Socialism: A Study in the Politics of Labour*, London, Allen & Unwin.

Nairn, T. (1964a) 'The English working class', *New Left Review* 24: 43-67.

Nairn, T. (1964b) 'The nature of the Labour Party, part one', *New Left Review* 27: 37-65.

Nairn, T. (1964c) 'The nature of the Labour Party, part two', *New Left Review* 28: 33-62.

Rutherford, J. (2011) 'The future is conservative', in Glasman, M., Rutherford, J., Stears, M. and White, S. (eds.) *The Labour Tradition and the Politics of Paradox*, London, the Oxford London Seminars/Soundings.

Thompson, E. P. (1961) '*The Long Revolution*: review', Parts I & II, *New Left Review* 9 & 10: 24-33 & 34-9.

Williams, R. (1958) *Culture and Society 1780-1950*, London, Chatto and Windus.

Williams, R. (1961) *The Long Revolution*, London, Pelican.

Williams, R. (ed.) (1968) *The May Day Manifesto 1968*, London, Penguin.

Notes

1. Exceptions are Jackson (2007) and Foote (1985).
2. The first version was published in 1967 as *New Left May Day Manifesto*. An expanded version appeared as a Penguin special the following year (Williams, 1968).

The Labour Party and the New Left

The first New Left, Blue Labour and English modernity

Jonathan Rutherford

This essay is about the first New Left and Blue Labour. They are both examples of emergent currents of thinking and action at times of political hiatus on the left. In this hiatus what counts is not policy but the energy of emerging political moods and intellectual currents. They begin to re-orientate thinking and action, reconfiguring existing political fault-lines, and once more connecting people with political agency. Policy follows.

The first New Left and Blue Labour are different in their politics, but they share a common historical thread. They mark the beginning and the closing of a specific historical period. It begins with the changes in economy and society in the 1950s, the social liberal revolution of the 1960s, and the historical defeat of the left in the neo-liberal economic revolution of Margaret Thatcher in 1979. It closes in 2008 with the self-destruction of this economic revolution and the subsequent unfolding revelations of deceit and corrupt behaviour in political, civic and commercial life.

The first New Left began in 1956, 57 years ago. It emerged out of the decline of the post-war welfare consensus, and the rise of a new kind of consumer capitalism. Its key figures were Edward Thompson, Raphael Samuel, Stuart Hall, Raymond Williams, Richard Hoggart, Charles Taylor and Alasdair MacIntyre. It lasted six years and after its demise they continued their work, creating a significant body of political and cultural thinking and philosophy.

Blue Labour emerged out of the self-destruction of the neo-liberal revolution and the search within the Labour Party for a viable political and economic alternative. It was conceived by Maurice Glasman in 2009 and was carried forward by a small group of politicians and academics. It had an extraordinary impact both within and outside the Labour Party, stimulating debate and often polarising opinion. In 2011 it crash landed. Those involved dusted themselves down and carried on.

What do these two intellectual movements tell us about the social and economic liberal revolutions in English society and politics over the last 57 years? And why does it matter to a Labour Party, which in 2010 suffered arguably its worst election defeat since 1918? These are the questions I address in this essay.

1956 and the first New Left

The first New Left emerged at a conjunction of historical trends. 1956 was the year of Krushchev's 'secret speech' and the Soviet invasion of Hungary, which broke the dominance of the Communist Party of Great Britain over a whole cohort of left-leaning intellectuals in Britain, and opened up the space for an independent, extra-parliamentary left. Edward Thompson and John Saville began publishing their cyclostyled journal, *The Reasoner*. Both were expelled from the Party, and in 1957 they launched *The New Reasoner*, one of the two journals associated with the first New Left.

1956 was the year of the post-imperial humiliation of Suez. The long Victorian age of Empire was drawing to a close. The Windrush generation of Caribbean migrants was a new presence, marking the beginning of a post-colonial and multicultural English society. The post-war years had seen the creation of a welfare state and a social democratic consensus. The consensus was the achievement of a long historical struggle by the counter-movement to laissez-faire capitalism, and it indicated an era drawing to a close. A period of sustained affluence was changing the culture and aspirations of the industrial working class. New forms of production and consumption were reconfiguring class relations. The cultural and social foundations of the labour movement were starting to erode. What next for the Labour Party?

In 1956 Anthony Crosland published an answer in his *The Future of Socialism*. He did so by partially dismissing the question. He said the post-war welfare settlement was permanent and capitalism had been transformed. 'Is this still capitalism?', he asked, and answered: 'No' (Crosland, 2006 [1956], 46). *The Future of Socialism* became the inspiration for future generations of Labour social democrats, but it also defined the limitations of this strand of Labour thinking, not only around political economy, but also culture.

Crosland signalled this warning in his final few pages on 'Liberty and gaiety in private life' and on 'Cultural and amenity planning'. He concluded by calling for a reaction against the austerity of the Fabian tradition through the pursuit of pleasure, beauty, personal freedom and enjoyment. It was almost an afterthought to his social democratic text and it was in this afterthought that the first New Left took root. The New Left was independent and democratic, radical in its critique of capitalism, and committed to the transformation of everyday cultural and social life. It rejected both orthodox communism and Fabianism.

The first New Left prefigured the rise of new class fractions created by the growth in higher education, the public sector, and a service economy. This new class fraction would burst onto the scene in the 1960s, rebelling against the older generation in a social liberal revolution in individuality and moral values. In 1957, Stuart Hall and others published the first issue of *The Universities and Left Review*. Its editorial confirmed the identity of the first New Left as an emergent politics, both in and against Labour: 'The age of orthodoxies has, once again, been outstripped by historical events … The thaw is on: but the landscape is still littered with the remnants and ruins of the political ice-age' (Hall et al., 1957).

The first New Left was the inheritor of an English high cultural arc, described by Jed Esty in his insightful book, *Shrinking Island* (2003), which began in the early years of the twentieth century with the Bloomsbury set. This included: the literary modernism of Virginia Woolf, which questioned the capacity of traditional forms of narrative to depict contemporary life; post-impressionism and its project of representing the world of feelings and the symbolic; and the liberalism that infused English elite culture, but which was in political decline with the rise of the Labour-voting working class. These trends came together in the political economy of John Maynard Keynes, who understood that a shared set of national cultural values, even elite ones, is a strong defence against the ideology of laissez-faire.

This high cultural arc of the inter-war years was a response to imperial decline, and a turn away from overseas and back to England. It was a response prevalent in the more traditional pastoralism of the Georgian poets and the English nationalism of G. K. Chesterton and Hilaire Belloc. The question, as T. S. Eliot put it in his poem *Little Gidding*, was how to portray human life in culture and society, 'Now and in England'. In 1932 it found a proselytiser in F. R. Leavis' *New Criticism* and the idea that 'Great Literature' promoted the possibilities of life. This English cultural renaissance and its literary canon was the inheritance of the post-war generation.

Culture as a resource

In 1957, Richard Hoggart's *The Uses of Literacy* attempted to turn this arc towards a democratic English working class culture. In 1958 Raymond Williams' essay 'Culture is ordinary' (Williams, 2001 [1958]) rejected the idea of culture as an elite aesthetic. Williams' anthropological approach to culture, as the practices and expression of life being lived, can be traced back through D. H. Lawrence, John Ruskin, and English romanticism to Samuel Coleridge and his idea of society and the 'cultivation of our humanity'.

It is a cultural tradition that shapes English modernity as both radical and conservative, and at odds with Enlightenment rationalism and the avant-garde of continental modernism. As much about moral sentiments and sensibility as it is about reason, it encompasses Edmund Burke as well as John Ruskin and William Morris. Morris' radical conservatism is a catalyst that brought together the literary first New Left and Edward Thompson's Marxist humanism in the historical recovery of the radical traditionalism of the English working class.

It is an English modernity of virtue, humanism, and democratic common culture. A modernity that is, in Williams' 1961 phrase, 'a long revolution' that 'requires new ways of thinking and feeling, new conceptions of relationships' (Williams, 1971 [1961], 13). But in this reworking of traditional English culture, Williams and Thompson in particular were not I think fully attuned to the disruptive power of the post-colonial conjuncture they found themselves in. During this period, they were not able to secure an internally coherent narrative of either their own project of modernity, or of England's national identity.

The first New Left's post-colonialism and internationalism revealed its paradoxical relationship to England. Stuart Hall describes his arrival at Oxford: 'Three months at Oxford persuaded me that it was not my home. I'm not English and I never will be. The life I have lived is one of partial displacement' (Hall, 2012). A life of partial displacement and cultural dislocation exemplifies the trajectory of the first New Left: Thompson's family past in India; the liminal class experience of the grammar school boys, Williams and Hoggart; Charles Taylor as a Canadian outsider. It believed in the value of popular culture and the idea of culture as ordinary, but it remained a critical outsider. The first New Left was a project of radical modernisation and the recovery of a democratic culture, but it couldn't be part of what it sought to make, and it did not belong to what it was attempting to recover.

The first New Left was both in and against Labour, and separate from mainstream politics. It spoke for the historical specificity of an emergent generational class fraction rather than a contested people. By the late 1960s it would be associated with the new counter cultures and a rejection of the virtues of class traditions and patrimony; an intergenerational conflict played out in countless families up and down the country. Partial displacement was also to become a domestic experience.

The second New Left

The first New Left lacked the theoretical resources to work through its indeterminacy. Thompson's humanism was not enough to explain the differentiations of culture and identity, nor to provide a convincing analysis of the complexity of historical change. It had on the one hand the inheritance of the Leavisite literary criticism it was trying to escape from, and on the other the crude Marxism it had rejected. Leavis, despite his faults, won out. Williams drew on the social anthropology of Ruth Benedict, and the social psychology of George Mead. J. K. Galbraith and C. Wright Mills were important influences. Charles Taylor initiated a communitarian engagement with Marx's theory of alienation in his 'Economic and Philosophical Manuscripts' of 1844 (Taylor, 1958). But these theoretical resources could not secure a coherent historical, political project for the first New Left.

In 1960, *The New Reasoner* and *The Universities and Left Review* merged to form *New Left Review* with Stuart Hall as editor. The emphasis was on understanding the cultural and economic conjuncture. Within two years the editorship had passed to the young Perry Anderson. Together with the academic Tom Nairn, Anderson developed an analysis of England's modernity and its class relations which made a decisive theoretical break with the first New Left.

The byword of Anderson and Nairn is the certainty of their own historical analysis. English society is, in Nairn's words, not much more than an 'impenetrable blanket of complacency' (Nairn, 1964, 36). England's intellectual life is a 'comprehensive, coagulated conservatism … for which England has justly won an international reputation' (Anderson, 1964, 40). Imperialism has left English modernity with an absent centre hollowed out by cultural philistinism and Benthamite utilitarianism. History, the future, intellectual rigour, an understanding of the totality of social relations, the historical political project: all lie across the Channel in continental Marxism and theory.

This transfer of intellectual allegiance detached the second New Left from common English culture. For Anderson, English political life is little more than a 'supine bourgeoisie' that has produced a 'subordinate proletariat' (Anderson, 1964, 43). The English working class, the virtue of everyday life, the search for practical forms of democracy, the art of muddling through, the value of the parochial: all are dismissed by the abstractions of structuralism and Marxist theory.

In 1968, Stuart Hall took over the Birmingham Centre for Cultural Studies from Richard Hoggart, and in a number of ground-breaking studies of society and culture developed the first New Left collective project within the academy. Under Hall's leadership, the threads of New Left thinking were woven into the emergent social movements around race, sexuality and gender, and had a decisive influence on *Marxism Today* in the 1980s and 1990s. But the growing influence of the 'linguistic turn' of continental theory – structuralism, post-structuralism, Louis Althusser, Jacques Lacan, Michel Foucault – widened the gap between New Left intellectuals and mainstream politics.

The turn was a reaction to the 'expressive humanism' of the first New Left. Its ideas of 'experience' and the individual as a unitary and internally undifferentiated subject were considered illusions. The conditions of one's existence could only be 'lived' 'through the categories, classifications and frameworks of culture' (Hall, 1981, 29). Meaning is not fixed, but continually slipping its cultural moorings through a play of difference in which nothing can be guaranteed. Hall took this interpretation of culture into his reworking of Gramsci's politics of hegemony and his ground-breaking analysis of Thatcherism.

Theories of difference and identity provided an intellectual dynamo for the social liberal revolution around race, sexuality, and gender relations. They teased apart the existing fabric of meaning in a similar way to the disembedding of social relations by the second, economic liberal revolution of capitalism that followed. Literary deconstruction and the universalist nature of Rawlsian political theory had the same impact. They disentangle the subject from material, cultural locatedness and meaningful relationships. Political agency and common action dissolve away into signifiers and abstraction. This highly rationalistic intellectual culture took hold in the universities and played no small part in shaping the thinking of a generation of the political elite.

Labour and the legacy of the New Left

There have been two consequences of the direction the New Left took following the ending of its first period. The first consequence is that its influence, particularly in its second form, did not translate beyond its original class and generational specificity into the broader population. Its disdain for English modernity and common culture distanced the intellectual left from the political contest in England around who defined the country. The contest was subsequently won by the New Right and Margaret Thatcher. In Birmingham, in June 1970, Enoch Powell declared the country under attack from an enemy within. 'Race' and immigration would play a major role in the new battle for Britain (Powell, 1971). For Powell, the enemy within was the liberal elite, which controlled the media and political establishment and which had abandoned England to immigration and to those who hated her.

It is Powell, not Thatcher, who is the political architect of the second, economic, liberal revolution. He laid claim to post-imperial England as a country betrayed. The Conservatives define the dominant English conservative imaginary. The left, pushed onto the back foot by populist resentment about immigration and the failure of Labour's economic modernisation, was increasingly drawn towards identity politics and cultural difference. 27 years later, when New Labour won the 1997 election, it still feared England as a reactionary country.

The second consequence is the fate of the Labour Party in the 1990s. The New Left was confined mostly to academics and intellectuals, who were not able to contest successfully the rising influence of the Third Way social democracy which accommodated itself to the second, economic liberal revolution. The Third Way mixture of social liberalism and economic liberalism led to a post-national cosmopolitanism which tended to valorise novelty, the global and change, over the ordinary, the local, and belonging. Like its academic cousin post-modernism, it had the effect of flattening out time, space and the hierarchy of values, helping to clear social and cultural impediments to commodification.

The first, social liberal revolution created a powerful trend towards a 'liberation ethic' of individual self-expression, anti-establishment sentiment, emotional attunement to the world, and the personal pursuit of pleasure. But these were also important resources for creating the new regimes of capital accumulation of the second, economic liberal revolution that followed in its wake. This second liberal revolution proceeded to restructure individual self-expression and desires around the deracinated economic rights and market freedoms of rational self-interest. What had begun as a politics of emancipation was appropriated into a culture of entitlement and winner-takes-all.

Blue Labour in One Nation

Over this period the political class ceded power and initiative to the market. Faced with a major systemic crisis the political class has sunk into inertia. The left fares no better. The crisis in capitalism has left it drifting in a state of political and cultural malaise. New

Labour in government was defined by the two liberal revolutions of the period. In consequence, it is associated in the public mind with excess – excessive levels of private debt, too much micro-managing government, too much immigration, inflated house prices, too much welfare, and too much money spent for too little return. There is a popular loss of trust in the capacity of the political class to contain this excess and restore a virtuous order. The economic crisis reverberates with a sense of blame, dispossession, and social insecurity as people react to the erosion of the cultural meanings, fidelities, and solidarities that bind them together in society.

Blue Labour is a response to the social and economic costs of the two liberal revolutions and to the crisis of Labour's meaning and purpose in the wake of the failure of Third Way social democracy. Like the first New Left, it is an attempt to frame a specifically English modernity rooted in the radical and conservative traditions of common life. And like the first New Left it has arrived on the threshold of a new era of economic development, but one whose society has been damaged by too much uncontrolled change and marketisation. If the first New Left was intent on uprooting the confining social conventions and homogenous culture of the past, Blue Labour is intent on putting down social and cultural roots for a common good.

Jonathan Rutherford is Emeritus Professor of Cultural Studies at Middlesex University.

References

Anderson, P. (1964) 'Origins of the present crisis', *New Left Review* 23: 26-53.

Crosland, C. A. R. (2006 [1956]) *The Future of Socialism*, London, Constable.

Esty, J. (2003) *Shrinking Island*, Princeton, Princeton University Press.

Hall, S. (1981) 'Cultural studies: two paradigms', in Bennett, T. et al. (eds.) *Culture, History and Social Process*, Milton Keynes, Open University Press.

Hall, S., Pearson, G., Samuel, R. and Taylor, C. (1957) 'Editorial', *Universities and New Left Review* 1 (1), archived at www.amielandmelburn.org.uk.

Hall, S. and Williams, Z. (2012) 'The Saturday interview', *Guardian* 11.2.2012.

Hoggart, R. (1957) *The Uses of Literacy*, London, Chatto and Windus.

Nairn, T. (1964) 'The nature of the Labour Party, part two', *New Left Review* 28: 33-62.

Powell, E. (1971) speech, reprinted in Wood, J. (ed.) *Powell and the 1970 Election*, Kingswood, Elliott Right Way Books.

Taylor, C. (1958) 'Alienation and community', *Universities and Left Review* 1 (5): 11-18, archived at www.amielandmelburn.org.uk.

Williams, R. (2001 [1958]) 'Culture is ordinary', reprinted in Higgins, J. (ed.) *The Raymond Williams Reader*, Oxford, Blackwell.

Williams, R. (1971 [1961]) *The Long Revolution*, London, Pelican Books.

Faith, flag and the 'first' New Left: E. P. Thompson and the politics of 'one nation'

Michael Kenny

The New Left has made a rather unexpected comeback in current political discourse, catching the interest of figures associated with Ed Miliband's leadership of the Labour Party, notably the Chair of its Policy Review, Jon Cruddas, and his collaborator Jonathan Rutherford (1). For those involved in the New Left, especially its early phase when it was a movement of people as well as ideas, this sudden renewal of interest is probably a surprise (for accounts of the early years of the New Left see Linn, 1993; Kenny, 1995). For while the New Left was for forty years one of the major intellectual engines on the British left, since the 1990s it has all but disappeared from view, retreating behind the walls of its one surviving institution, the heavyweight journal *New Left Review* (*NLR*).

The main motivation for today's interest is a search for intellectual roots on behalf of today's communitarian and patriotic proponents of 'One Nation Labour'. Cruddas has expressed his own solidarity with the ideas of the New Left 'mark 1', notably its attempt to recuperate English cultural traditions, and his alienation from the New Left 'mark 2', when, under the influence of Perry Anderson, the emphasis turned to the wholesale importation of continental Marxist theory into the supposedly conservative cultural backwaters of Britain.

One important question posed by this renewal of interest is whether such a 'Cain and Abel' picture of the New Left represents an accurate representation of what some see as a more singular and evolving current than the language of 'first' and 'second' New Lefts suggests (Davis, 2006). Another related question – which is the main issue I want to explore in this essay – is what the attempt to reclaim English traditions, which formed one of the key impulses within the early New Left, offers to those interested in fleshing out further the intellectual dimensions of a 'One Nation' approach. In order to do so, I consider the thinking of one of the iconic figures within the early New Left, whose work appears to fit best with the 'New Left mark 1' model – that of the historian, activist and intellectual Edward Thompson. I conclude that his work does indeed supply a valuable and stimulating guide for today's progressive patriots, and explore the challenging insights he provided into the political character of progressive patriotism.

The 'first' New Left

The first phase of the New Left movement was home to a variety of contending impulses and ideas, some of which were decidedly wary of the radical patriotism advocated by figures associated with *The New Reasoner* (*NR*) journal in which Thompson was prominently involved after 1958 (Kenny, 1995). Literary critic and cultural theorist Raymond Williams, whose major work, *Culture and Society*, published in 1958, also fits with the radical-patriotic template, subsequently renounced this kind of approach and moved towards a more Marxist-inflected mode of critical thinking. And Stuart Hall, another major figure from the early New Left, became a consistent critic of the imperial mindset and ethno-cultural residues that infused English national identity, and has remained sceptical about the prospects of reclaiming the national past for progressive ends (Hall, 2012).

The leading figure within this current whose work does appear most congruent with the image of the first New Left projected by Cruddas is the historian and activist Edward Thompson. His major intellectual dispute during the 1960s with the young intellectual and critic Perry Anderson, and his talented collaborator Tom Nairn, provides important evidence for the contention that a fundamental schism over the values of patriotism and the nation were indeed central to the different phases and factions of the New Left.

Below, I revisit the main issues at stake in that dispute. In particular, I explore the terms of Thompson's rejoinder to the cosmopolitan Marxism proposed by Anderson and Nairn, and point to his emphasis on the left's need to embrace lived experience and the democratic capacities of ordinary people. I also consider those facets of Thompson's position which offer an interesting supplement to current forms of progressive patriotism. In particular I examine his highly political account of the nature of the struggle over the national past, which is in important respects quite different to the call of figures like Paul Kingsnorth (1999) for the re-discovery of an authentic and endangered English past. For Thompson, the national story needed to be re-fashioned as much as re-located.

The Thompson-Anderson dispute recalled

The major intellectual and political dispute that erupted between Thompson and Anderson was one of a number of prominent theoretical disagreements in which New Left thinkers were embroiled during the 1960s and 1970s. Yet this particular argument stood out both for the quality and clarity of the contributions it elicited on both sides, which gave expression to deeply embedded tendencies within intellectual life in general and socialist thinking in particular.

At one level, this was a disagreement about the nature of the New Left itself, and its most precious asset and visible presence – *NLR*. Thompson had been one of the two editors of the *NR*, which had provided a major gathering point for former Communists who had left the party in disgust after the Soviet invasion of 1956, as well as for Labour sympathisers in search of new ideas and inspiration. After months of often difficult negotiations, *NR* merged with a very different publication – the more metropolitan and theoretically orientated *Universities and Left Review* (*ULR*) – and *NLR* first appeared in 1960.

Although he was the obvious candidate for the position, Thompson opted not to become its inaugural editor. Instead, this role went to the talented (though inexperienced) Stuart Hall, then a doctoral student at Oxford University who had been integral to the work of the *ULR*. Thompson identified closely with the political mission of the new journal, which set out with considerable ambition to bridge the chasms that tended to bedevil socialist politics – between theory and practice, culture and politics, and parliamentary party and broader movement. And, though he was disappointed with what he deemed to be the lightweight content of some of its early issues, Thompson had committed a good deal to the New Left, and was convinced that it had a future as a political, not just intellectual venture.

But the new journal was plagued by the perennial nightmare of left periodicals lacking wealthy benefactors – the lack of a stable financial base. Anderson emerged as the journal's potential saviour, a role that his own wealthy background enabled him to play.

What began as a delicate negotiation between him and the *NLR* Board ended in acrimony, with Thompson feeling that a coup of sorts had taken place, and most others seeing Anderson as the only choice available if the journal was to survive.

Anderson assumed the position of editor in 1962. Most of the Editorial Board left soon after, and were replaced with more sympathetic figures. The *NLR* was now launched on a very different course, based upon Anderson's own interpretation of the peculiar path of British historical development and his unyielding sense of the intellectual deficiencies of the British left.

The arguments that figured in his public exchange with Thompson were in fact anticipated by disagreements that had been aired for some time on the journal's Board, and which erupted acrimoniously at a two-day meeting it held in April 1963. Thompson launched his own intellectual ballistic missile, in the shape of a 15,000 word memorandum circulated to the *NLR* Board in advance of this key meeting (Hamilton, 2011, 102-5). No longer prepared to hold his tongue, he set out with a brutal clarity his objections to the theoretical focus that Anderson had instilled. His polemic provided the guts of the controversial and combative essay he later published in a different left periodical – 'The peculiarities of the English' – as *NLR* refused to publish his trenchant critique of its political and intellectual direction.

In this piece he set out a refutation of Anderson's and Nairn's controversial account of Britain's historical development, and their sweeping dismissal of its labour movement and intellectual culture. The debate touched on some iconic topics, including the role and character of theory, and its relation with practice; how socialist ideas related to national cultures and traditions; and how the left should engage with a polity – Britain – which felt so conservative and un-modern.

Returning to these arguments now is to re-visit a completely different intellectual atmosphere, one where theoretically informed, but accessible, arguments carried a sense of significance that is almost unimaginable now. While Anderson's brand of Marxism fell into abeyance in political terms after the 1970s, his confident expression of socialism in universalist terms, and his readiness to characterise those championing indigenous radicalism as, at best, backward-looking romantics, left an indelible imprint upon subsequent generations of socialist thought.

It was not until the 1990s that the idea that nationhood and patriotism might be important themes for progressives to engage with was taken seriously again. But even then, the dominant voices of liberal and socialist theory were cosmopolitan, not national, and Britain was largely written off by intellectuals and New Labour politicians as a brand that was desperately in need of a make-over (Berry and Kenny, 2013).

The Anderson/Nairn thesis

Anderson's and Nairn's famous historical interpretation of Britain's blocked assent to modernity, and its creaking, pre-modern state system, reflected their considerable emphasis on the exceptional nature of its historical development. The class compromise that had been forged between a declining aristocracy and rising bourgeoisie had bequeathed an unusually insular and tradition-bound culture. Their additional characterisation of the supine and anti-intellectual nature of the labour movement in Britain, and their dismissal of the tepid reformism and 'trade union consciousness' manifested in the Labour Party, reflected their belief that the British left was uniquely hampered by the appearance in the early decades of the nineteenth century of a radical movement that pre-dated the arrival of Marxist theory from the continent. Intellectuals only moved towards radical politics, and the fledgling labour movement, at the very end of the nineteenth century, and those few thinkers who were influential upon the development and thinking of the Labour Party were, they argued, pseudo-intellectuals who helped embed a conservative reformism within the party (see Anderson, 1963; 1965; 1966; 1968; and Nairn, 1964a).

In an influential later analysis that built upon these foundations, Nairn proceeded to diagnose the culture of 'Labourism' which had become the governing ethos of the party (Nairn, 1964b; 1964c). This consisted of a set of values which rendered the Labour Party unwilling to break from the culture associated with the routines and rituals of parliament, and a tendency to focus on piecemeal issues while eschewing more radical ambitions. The embedded nature of Labourism, he argued, meant that Labour failed to develop an alternative social philosophy to that associated with the dominant assumptions of the economic and political systems of the day. Their argument carried strong echoes of the critique developed by Ralph Miliband, father of Ed and David, and an important figure at this time in the New Left, whose own often difficult relationship with Thompson has been fully chronicled (Newman, 2002). It was a standard assumption of progressive intellectuals in the 1960s and 1970s that Labour was so infused by the assumptions of the archaic British state and its dominant classes that it was highly unlikely to act as the midwife for an advance towards socialism (Miliband, 1961).

Professional historians have for the most part joined with Thompson in questioning many of these thinkers' particular arguments, and decrying their heavy reliance upon modern France as the 'norm' against which British exceptionalism was critically gauged. Anderson and Nairn stressed the unwillingness of the bourgeoisie to break with the aristocratic interest and lead the modernisation of British state and society as the defining aspect of the British experience. The English capitalist class, they argued, was uniquely conservative, and was mirrored by an intelligentsia that was unable to articulate a comprehensive critique of a society that was suspended between the *ancien régime* and a modern industrial order.

This supine and parochial bourgeoisie induced similar characteristics, they argued, in the working class and its culture. The lack of any major body of indigenous social thought was reflected in the anti-intellectual prejudices that were embedded throughout the labour movement. What Thompson and the early New Left praised as important instances of anti-capitalist protest – including the romantic artists whom Thompson admired so greatly, or the critics of industrialism praised by Raymond Williams in *Culture and Society* (1958) – were, for Anderson and Nairn, symptoms of an ingrained conservatism which looked back to a mythic past rather than seeking to construct an alternative socialist future.

In his subsequent work Nairn (1977) took this analysis further, arguing that the English had fatefully proved unable to imagine themselves as a nation, preferring to divest their sovereignty to the arcane institutions and ethos of the state-form that was devised for the internal and external empires which Britain governed. In place of a modern, democratic sense of nationality there arose only pathological and reactionary manifestations of a stalled English consciousness.

These ideas provided much of the intellectual framework for the later New Left's analysis of British politics. Anderson's and Nairn's highly critical account of the Labour Party rested upon what one critic termed its 'Olympian' (Sedgwick, 1964) understanding of the relationship between intellectuals and the everyday lives and ordinary experiences of workers. Social theory, they argued, came from minds that were unencumbered by the national-cultural traditions of the societies they put under the microscope. The changes Anderson introduced to the *NLR* exemplified this vision, as it removed itself almost entirely from any connection with political life, and disavowed what remained of the New Left as a social movement.

Thompson's rehabilitation of the English tradition

This stance represented a major departure from the thinking of their New Left predecessors. Thompson and others involved with the *NR* had made clear their belief that the radical traditions of the labour movement, its collective sense of solidarity and reciprocity, and the rich ethos of self-reliance and democratic commitment upon which it was built, ought to be the left's lodestar. Though somewhat split on the political question of what kind of relationship to the Labour Party the New Left ought to adopt, figures from this circle were for the most part engaged, critical, friends of the labour movement, not distant and unsparing rejectionists.

Thompson's riposte to Anderson and Nairn, set out in his iconic essay 'The peculiarities of the English' (1965), represented the most developed reflection from within the ranks of the early New Left. He defended this current's desire to re-connect with indigenous cultural traditions and the efforts it had made to challenge established ideas about the national past. He also lambasted the sweeping critique of the parochialism and conservatism of the labour movement put forward by Anderson and Nairn. The detached, bird's eye view which their theoretical analysis promoted meant that they were unable to grasp the concrete and contingent nature of the traditions and struggles out of which Labour had emerged. Thompson noted too the lack of a considered sense of the balance of forces at work within their historical account. Any sense of politics as the 'art of the possible' was entirely absent within such thinking.

His objections were to surface once more in the course of his double-barrelled response to the ultra-rationalism at the heart of the structuralist philosophy peddled by the French Marxist theorist Louis Althusser in the 1970s (Thompson, 1978). His abstruse and decidedly anti-humanist thinking sparked considerable interest in left circles, appealing to those who, following Anderson's lead, were attracted to theoretical projects that were the very mirror-image of English empiricism.

Thompson lamented the rationalist fallacy at the heart of these bodies of thinking, which claimed to be able to detect the laws of motion at work within history by adopting the vantage point of the detached observer, equipped with the apparatus and methodology supplied by a pseudo-scientific Marxism. In the memorandum he sent round the Board of *NLR* in 1963, he complained about the tendency of the new generation of Marxist intellectuals to write off the war of position that was quietly being waged on the domestic scene, and astutely noted the tendency of such figures to be seduced by the more dramatic and exciting developments happening across the Channel:

> While we strain to catch the idioms of the Third World, of Paris, of Poland, of Milan, might there not be a growing discourse around us, pregnant with possibilities, not only for us but for other peoples? (Quoted in Elliott, 1998, 32)

The substantive basis for Thompson's objections to such thinking was elaborated more fully and famously in the powerful 'The poverty of theory' (1978), in which he skewered Althusserian thinking and reprised his arguments against Anderson and Nairn. In this, one of his finest essays, he wrote as a self-confident and widely known intellectual who was not afraid to deride the latest instance in the British left's inglorious history of falling for theoretical sophistry and the odd guru. Swiftian satire and savage wit intermingled with heavyweight intellectual argument as he lambasted Althusser's theoretical apparatus and attacked those, including the later New Left, who had taken seriously such amoral dogma. This was socialism turned into a kind of secular theology, the intellectual corollary, he argued, of a Stalinist approach to politics.

Just as importantly, Thompson elaborated his understanding of the significance of lived experience. He regarded this as both an intellectual and a moral category, which socialist thinking had to honour and engage, not dismiss as a site where ideological hegemony was inexorably secured. Ordinary people, he argued, were much more than the passive recipients of structurally rooted processes. It was the culturally mediated ways in which they made sense of the circumstances they faced, and their attempts to transcend these, as well as the traditions they called upon in order to do so, that needed to be at the heart of historical understanding and progressive thought.

And, as he demonstrated in the path-breaking work that he published in the early 1960s, *The Making of the English Working Class* (1963), and in an important set of later essays on the eighteenth century (which are collected in Thompson, 2009), in the English case it was often by invoking pre-modern forms of understanding, including myths, pieces of folklore and ideas about customary right, that 'the people' gradually became aware of their distinct interests and needs in relation to the ruling classes.

Elsewhere, Thompson justified and explored the importance to English radicals of a love of country. His was a patriotism that did not replicate or mimic that favoured by the political right, but actively sought to contest the ways in which 'the *patria*' was understood in the popular mind, and strove to inflect the political conclusions that people would derive from patriotic sentiments. That Thompson enjoyed such a high standing in socialist circles while advocating the importance of faith and flag, both of which were anathema to large parts of the left, says much about his skills and credibility as a historian and left-wing intellectual.

But, importantly, he was clear that the traditions and institutions that were passed down to the present did not deserve to be venerated merely because they were there, as Burkean logic suggested. Instead, Thompson argued, they mattered because of the sense of agency and meaning that ordinary people were able to derive from them. An apprecia-tion of the cultural dimensions of political struggle, and of the inspirational role played by those who sometimes challenged the norms and morals of their various communities, arose from the kind of independently-minded, historical sensibility he promoted. Community, custom and tradition were blended, in his very English outlook, with the virtues of independence, rebelliousness and self-realisation. A sense of the importance of the 'common life' needs, in Thompsonian terms, to be balanced against a respect for the capacities and desire of ordinary people to gain control of their own circumstances and to devise forms of self-government.

In his eyes, therefore, the patriotism of the left was in a perpetual struggle with that which coursed through the conservative imagination. He disliked the Tory fetish for the core institutions of the British state, identifying strongly with the cause of political reform, which he located as a cornerstone of working-class radicalism, not, as has more recently become the view, as a disposable luxury that distracted from 'real' issues. Established traditions were to be actively engaged and continually remade and refined, not swallowed whole. Reclaiming English culture and customs for a progressive kind of politics therefore involved the combined exercise of countless individual wills and imaginations, and implied a willingness by radicals to tackle the inequalities of power, wealth and status which were fortified by conservative accounts of the nation.

There was a clear echo in all this of Italian theorist Antonio Gramsci's concept of the 'national popular', and, at various points in his writing, he signalled his admiration for

Gramsci's work. For both of them, the rich and diverse cultures of the nation provided the soil in which socialist attitudes might grow – though there was nothing automatic or inevitable about this process. The historical past, and the different interpretations to which it was subjected, were vital parts of the territory upon which the left needed to conduct its imaginative and cultural struggles.

For Thompson, the left was best placed when it combined a romantic appreciation of the values of community and everyday life with a post-Enlightenment commitment to the determination of ordinary people to develop their own capacities and, with them, collective forms of agency. Desire and reason were the driving forces that made a sense of commonality and agency blossom among those at the bottom of the pile. The working class, he famously argued, made itself as much as it was made.

What One Nation Labour can learn from Thompson

Although fifty years have now passed since the publication of his major work, *The Making of the English Working Class*, Thompson's thinking continues to possess a considerable resonance. And this is especially true now that many on the left are once more recoiling from rationalistic and cosmopolitan forms of thinking – most recently associated with the New Labour years.

But, importantly, he supplemented this appreciation with an insistence that traditions and institutions were to be actively re-engaged and, if necessary, altered and challenged, not simply accepted and venerated. The correct alternative to the cosmopolitanism and rationalism which were abiding temptations of left intellectuals and policy thinkers was not, Thompson argued, a retreat to the imagined community of the pre-industrial village, but vigorous and inspiring efforts to re-tell the national story in ways that illuminated the contributions and struggles of ordinary men and women. He pointed towards a politics etched in the vernacular of hope, informed by a vision that was both radical and romantic in its inclinations.

The left needed to be weaned off its penchant for abstract, theoretical schemes, and reminded of the need to engage and understand the richness and complexity of the everyday lives of ordinary people. Anderson and Nairn were the latest in a long line of clever thinkers who, as Orwell had sharply noted, had come to view their own national culture as parochial and backward, while lauding that of other European states as inherently more impressive and progressive. This remains a salutary observation in a context where many current commentators see only pathology and chauvinism at the heart of the celebration of Englishness, while praising to the skies the nationalism of the Scots and the Welsh.

Jon Cruddas is right, therefore, to suppose that the thinking of parts of the early New Left ought to be recalled and engaged by today's 'One Nation' thinkers. Re-considering Thompson's writings and his New Left arguments, in particular, brings us into contact with some subtly different ways of reflecting upon contemporary debates about nationhood and the national past.

For Thompson showed above all how progressive patriotism was different in kind to forms of Englishness that were insular and isolationist in character. In his view, grounding progressive politics in the soil of the English *patria* was intimately connected to the idea of developing forms of solidarity and co-operation with allies and movements beyond England. Throughout his political life, Thompson prioritised the development of connections and the exchange of ideas with European radicals and socialists, including those labouring under the yoke of Soviet-style socialism (who were for the most part ignored or forgotten by Western socialists during the Cold War). He did so out of a sense of Britain as a generous, confident and outward-looking country, whose peoples' destiny was intimately connected to the fate of other parts of Europe.

These commitments were most movingly revealed in one of his lesser known works, a short account of his brother Frank Thompson's death, fighting at the behest of the Special Operations Executive alongside Bulgarian partisans against the Germans during the Second World War (Thompson, 1997). This homage to his much admired elder sibling serves – as is true of so many of Thompson's portraits of historical characters – as an exemplar. This was progressive patriotism in action – fully engaged with the struggles for freedom elsewhere, and confidently rooted in a pride in the English heritage.

Edward's own formative experiences, including his role as a tank commander with British forces in the Second World War, and his leading role in the European anti-nuclear movement of the 1980s, also exemplified these deeply-held commitments. So, while he was unashamed about his love of England's literary and cultural heritage, he was equally clear that English patriotism was at its best confident and outward-facing, not sour and insular. The England of his imagination was quite typically conservative in its cultural tastes, left-wing in its politics, and generously liberal in its approach to other cultures and peoples.

A second, striking lesson embodied in his work concerns his strong sense that the language and ethos of nationhood needed to be understood as deeply embroiled within political struggles, not as alternatives to the strategic dilemmas and conflicts that politics involves. In order to develop a radical politics that was true to England, the national past had to be respected, engaged, and actively re-interpreted. A sense of agency – of an imaginative and historical kind – was the hallmark of a progressive patriotism. And, in his mind, this was quite the opposite of a conservative veneration for the institutional conventions and norms of earlier eras.

A reconsideration now of the extraordinary body of historical writings and political essays that Thompson produced reveals how clear-minded he was in avoiding the false choice between grand theorising on the one hand, and a conservative vision of an insular and parochial England on the other. There have always been other, better positions for progressives to take. Thompson's work, like that of George Orwell before him, represents a valuable reminder of the richness of the English socialist imagination, and the considerable resources this lineage has bequeathed for later progressive patriots.

E. P. Thompson's unashamed love of country was interwoven with a strong commitment to England's dissenting and democratic heritage, as well as an unerring commitment to the merits of a common humanity. Above all, he advanced a highly political sense of the different values and ideals that a politics rooted in nationhood could supply. The radical *patria* arose out of the dream of a better society in which the power and wealth of the social and economic elites were challenged, decentralised and redistributed. There was always more than one imagined nation in play within political life, and it was the duty of the left to persuade, inspire and organise so that its patriotic and progressive version would ultimately win the day.

What then might Thompson have made of 'One Nation Labour'? I would guess that it would have left him interested but also on his guard. He would, I suspect, have been cheered that the language of patriotism was at the heart of Labour's sense of mission, but concerned if this slogan signalled too great an accommodation with political forms of conservatism. It was only by vigorously contesting this territory, and finding meanings and inspiration within it for a transformative politics in the here-and-now, that Thompson thought that the left would win the hearts and minds of the English people.

Michael Kenny is Professor of Politics at Queen Mary, University of London.

References

Anderson, P. (1963) 'Origins of the present crisis', *New Left Review* 23: 26-53.

Anderson, P. (1965) 'The left in the fifties', *New Left Review* 29: 3-18

Anderson, P. (1966) 'Socialism and pseudo-empiricism', *New Left Review* 35: 2-42.

Anderson, P. (1968) 'Components of the national culture', *New Left Review* 50: 3-57.

Berry, C. and Kenny, M. (2013) 'Ideologies, intellectuals and the nation', in Freeden, M., Sargent, L. T. and Stears, M. (eds.) *Oxford Handbook of Political Ideologies*, Oxford, Oxford University Press.

Chun, L. (1993) *The British New Left*, Edinburgh, Edinburgh University Press.

Cruddas, J. (2012) 'The role of the state in the good society', *New Statesman* 13.12.2012.

Davis, M. (2006) 'The Marxism of the British New Left', *Journal of Political Ideologies*, 11 (3): 335-58.

Elliott, G. (1998) *Perry Anderson: The Merciless Laboratory of History*, Minneapolis, University of Minnesota Press.

Hall, S. (2012) 'We need to talk about Englishness', *New Statesman* 23.8.2012.

Hamilton, S. (2011) *The Crisis of Theory: E. P. Thompson, the New Left and Post-War British Politics*, Manchester, Manchester University Press.

Kenny, M. (1995) *The First New Left: British Intellectuals after Stalin*, London, Lawrence and Wishart.

Kingsnorth, P. (1999) *Real England: The Battle Against the Bland*, London, Portobello Books.

Miliband, R. (1961) *Parliamentary Socialism: A Study in the Politics of Labour*, London, Allen and Unwin.

Nairn, T. (1964a) 'The English working class', *New Left Review* 24: 43-67.

Nairn, T. (1964b) 'The nature of the Labour Party, part one', *New Left Review* 27: 37-65.

Nairn, T. (1964c) 'The nature of the Labour Party, part two', *New Left Review* 28: 33-62.

Nairn, T. (1977) *The Break-Up of Britain*, London, New Left Books.

Newman, M. (2002) *Ralph Miliband and the Politics of the New Left*, London, Merlin.

Sedgwick, P. (1964) 'The two New Lefts', *International Socialism* 17: 15.

Thompson, E. P. (1963) *The Making of the English Working Class*, London, Penguin.

Thompson, E. P. (1965) 'The peculiarities of the English', *Socialist Register, 1965*: 311-62.

Thompson, E. P. (1978) 'The poverty of theory', in his *The Poverty of Theory and Other Essays*, London, Merlin.

Thompson, E. P. (1997) *Beyond the Frontier: The Politics of a Failed Mission: Bulgaria 1944*, London, Merlin.

Thompson, E. P. (2009) *Customs in Common*, London, Merlin.

Williams, R. (1958) *Culture and Society 1780-1950*, London, Chatto and Windus.

Note

1. These issues were considered at a conference on 'The Labour Party and the British New Left', held at Queen Mary, University of London, on 27 June 2012, at which both Cruddas and Rutherford were speakers. See also Cruddas (2012) and Jonathan Rutherford's article in this issue of *Renewal*.

The New Left's economic model: the challenge to Labour Party orthodoxy

Mark Wickham-Jones

Writing in *The Guardian* in 1987 about a retrospective conference, the Oxford scholar Brian Harrison reported that one member of the audience had pointed out that 'The New Left has never succeeded even in providing a coherent sketch of the socialist society that would compare in stature with Crosland's *The Future of Socialism*' (Harrison, 1987, 18). The point was reinforced with a photograph of Crosland accompanying the article and a strapline reading 'The New Left, outside the Labour Party, has nothing to offer compared with Anthony Crosland's sketch of a socialist society.' The proceedings of the same event published a comment by Lawrence Daly (1989), titled 'A miner's Bible', as part of its conference scrapbook. Talking about the New Left pamphlet, *A Socialist Wages Plan* (Alexander and Hughes, 1959), Daly, who had been General Secretary of the National Union of Mineworkers between 1968 and 1984, argued: 'It seemed to be everything I believed in. I was very much against mineworkers, or indeed any other workers, being paid purely on the basis of market forces.' He continued, 'Because I was so impressed by *A Socialist Wages Plan*, it became for a while my Bible as an activist in the coal mines.'

It is easy to see why the first view of the New Left has become so prevalent. In part, it is a reflection of the cultural, historical and foreign policy concerns articulated by its leading figures during the late 1950s: Stuart Hall, John Saville, E. P. Thompson and Raymond Williams spoke directly to such themes. The development of a comprehensive programme was also inhibited by disagreements amongst its leading figures over the movement's connection to Labour politics. In any case, the New Left was remarkably successful in speaking to a number of distinct and original issues at this time such as, for example, the relevance of sociological categories for reformist analyses and the extent of youthful disaffection with conventional politics. (The development of a network of clubs and coffee houses such as the Partisan in London assisted in the latter area). Given the circumstances in which the New Left emerged, the influence of the Soviet invasion of Hungary and the British incursion into Suez (both in 1956), it was to be expected that considerable attention would also be given over to foreign policy issues. At the time further consideration was granted to the United Kingdom's independent nuclear deterrent, an orientation that is equally unsurprising given the nature of the Campaign for Nuclear Disarmament and the accompanying crisis that engulfed Labour politics during this period. Of course, the relative affluence of the 1950s created uncertainties for left-wingers (see the discussion in Davis, 2012): how should they respond to apparent material prosperity? What issues should they focus upon? The definitive texts about the New Left (Chun, 1993; Kenny, 1995) have not neglected economic issues of the kind raised by *A Socialist Wages Plan* (the latter in particular devotes a chapter to such topics). But, given the considerations just noted, it is predictable that the focus of their attention has been on other matters. Indeed, an examination of contemporary discussions of the New Left, for example in the pages of *The Guardian* or *The Times* would lead to pretty much a straightforward conclusion. The New Left appeared to give little attention to economic issues and as such failed to develop a coherent model of social democracy.

By contrast, the revisionists within (and surrounding) the Labour Party offered an apparently strong and robust account of the reformist project. Tony Crosland's 1956 *The Future of Socialism* seemed, of course, the epitome of such an approach. Many commentators and participants concluded that this 540 page tome, published in October 1956 and weighing in at nearly two pounds, developed a complete analysis of British society (and its economy) as well as of the normative goals that should guide social democrats (for a critical discussion see Wickham-Jones, 2007). In it, long-held articles of faith for left-wing politics, most obviously nationalisation, were rejected as ineffective, irrelevant, and unpopular. In place of public ownership, Keynesian demand management and, at the level of the firm, a new managerial stratum would provide the basis for progressive policies. With regard to the latter, as a result of the managerial revolution that had separated ownership from control, a new layer of business executives would forsake profit maximisation in favour of other objectives. Power was dispersed throughout society: to government, to voters, to unions, and to managers, as well as, residually and insignificantly, to owners of capital. Firms could be taxed to generate a surplus to fund the social and welfare services that were required in the pursuit of equality (the defining goal of social democracy). It was not just nationalisation that Crosland jettisoned: he was lukewarm about planning and about any arrangement promoting industrial democracy. He suggested that there was no need to adopt an incomes policy or plan any growth in wages. Governments could rely, he claimed, on 'the sense and moderation of the unions' in this area (Crosland, 1956, 461).

The New Left challenge to revisionism

Against Crosland's model, the New Left sometimes looked disconnected and disorganised. To be sure, its members might adopt positions on particular topics but there was not much that might be considered as an all-inclusive programme. There was certainly no single volume either to challenge or to rival *The Future of Socialism*. However, whether such a failure means that the New Left did not articulate an economic model is less manifest. Many of the economic arguments deployed within the New Left are consistent, both with each other and in the challenge that they make towards revisionist doctrine. Many anticipate the concerns raised in later debates on the left during the 1970s and so helped shape the emergence of Labour's Alternative Economic Strategy (Wickham-Jones, 1996, 82). Such material tends to be found on that side of the New Left that was more supportive of Labour as a viable reformist agency; those who developed these points were more likely to be 'younger' members and, with the exception of Ken Alexander and John Hughes, to write for *Universities and Left Review* (*ULR*) rather than *The New Reasoner*.

Members of the New Left challenged Crosland across a range of issues. In one initiative, members of the New Left refuted Crosland's argument about the separation of ownership from control in modern capitalism. Based on painstaking research at Companies House in London, and drawing theoretical inspiration from the work of the American sociologist C. Wright Mills, they argued in the pamphlet *The Insiders* that, in contrast to the framework set out in *The Future of Socialism*, share owners and managers were part of an interlocking network (Hall et al., 1958). As a response to Labour's 1957 policy document, *Industry and Society* (a publication heavily influenced by revisionist thought), the authors of *The Insiders* made a number of claims. Significant, concentrated private shareholding remained. In any case there were strong links between shareholders and managers, many of whom owned equity in the firms in which they worked as well as in other private corporations. Together, shareholders and managers formed an interlocking network with multiple connections: 'Top managers, top directors, top shareholders, closely interlocked, are all, equally, the beneficiaries of the power, profits and prestige of the giant corporations' (Hall et al., 1958, ii). Personal wealth and power stemmed from the success of the business; in turn that meant that wealth and power were intimately related to profit, effectively the driver of the system. *The Insiders* argued: 'The salaries and perquisites of the managers and executives are merely new concealed forms of capital appreciation' (Hall et al., 1958, 31). The pamphlet piled on the criticisms of Crosland and of *Industry and Society*: oligopolistic firms faced little competition and could increase prices, thus generating inflation. They could pressure governments into making concessions on policy. Michael Barratt Brown (1958, 1959) followed up the analysis developed in *The Insiders* about the corporate networks and elites underpinning British capitalism with a series of papers in *ULR* entitled 'The Controllers'. Fifty years on *The Insiders* provides a powerful portrait of the elite character of British politics. It does not seem, however, to have had much impact at the time. The press did not pick up on it – there was no reference at all to it in *The Guardian* - and it does not seem to have generated much wider discussion.

The New Left also identified a structural imperative that shaped the capitalist economy. In an early issue of *New Left Review*, Charles Taylor argued that there were limits to the extent that Keynesian welfarism could be funded via a tax on profits: 'the motor of the system is after all profit, the private accumulation of capital. If we impose very heavy taxes, we are siphoning off the fuel from this motor. We cannot expect it to drive on regardless' (Taylor, 1960, 11). In the early 1960s, academic discussion about the nature of the firm raised the possibility that efficient capital markets meant firms had to maximise profits in order to sustain dividends and so avoid hostile takeovers, an essentially neo-classical proposition (see the later discussion in Singh, 1975). The New Left did not articulate such an argument explicitly; though in a talk at the Universities and Left Review Club in London in March 1958, the trade unionist Clive Jenkins (1958) argued that 'takeovers in US underline that managers can be displaced'. He claimed that in such circumstances profit maximisation remained central as companies 'search for the greatest returns'. Accordingly, 'prestige for managers [was] absolutely related to profitability and eventually to dividends.' The issue is notable because in *The Future of Socialism*, Crosland identified differences between capital markets in the United Kingdom and those found elsewhere in Europe countries. In many of the latter, especially in Germany – with 'the bare shadow of a free capital market' – alternative arrangements had developed to generate capital for investment (Crosland, 1956, 431). Having made the distinction about the nature of capital markets, Crosland did not follow it up. In a brief passage on takeovers, he did not discuss the impact of hostile bids on profit maximisation (Crosland, 1956, 354-7).

New Left authors accepted Crosland's claim that the British experience of nationalisation had been unsuccessful. However, they did not reject it as a policy intervention. Rather they indicated that it needed to be reworked and reformulated with a different structure and clearer criteria. When *The Guardian* accused the New Left of lacking originality, Stuart Hall complained: 'The unpopularity of nationalisation has to do with the form of public ownership to which the Labour Party has been committed since the Morrison era' (Hall, 1959, 4). It was 'bureaucratic and anonymous'; it suffocated the desire 'to participate directly' in the workplace. Moreover, the monopolistic nature of the economy and power of large private corporations meant public ownership remained relevant as a policy intervention. John Hughes (1960) argued that large firms were inegal-itarian, inefficient – they exploited their monopolistic status within the economy – and inflationary – they did not face price competition. Hughes claimed that the concentration of large firms in the economy led to stagnation. In such a context there was a straight-forward case for public ownership. It provided a means to control private firms whose production needed to be planned and stable and whose prices should be competitive. A central focus was the steel industry, whose nationalisation was the most contentious intervention undertaken by the 1945-51 Labour government, one that was subsequently reversed by the Conservatives. Hughes (1957) argued that renationalisation would make the industry accountable; help coordinate planning across the economy; and meet longer term goals. New Left authors also made the case for import restrictions and exchange controls. In order to plan national output, firms should discuss investment proposals with the government. Other contributors indicated the possibilities of workers' control, albeit in a slightly abstract manner (and an area that the Institute for Workers' Control developed much more fully a decade or so later). The authors of *The Insiders* argued: 'Public ownership must be seen in the context of the original socialist goal of industrial democracy' (Hall et al., 1958, 25).

It may be in the area of wages policy that the New Left offered its most distinctive contribution to the discussion of economic strategy (see Wickham-Jones, 2013). In the spring of 1959, Ken Alexander and John Hughes published *A Socialist Wages Plan*, the document that Lawrence Daly referred to so glowingly above. At the time the prevalent attitude within Labour, as articulated by Crosland, rejected incomes policies. By contrast, Alexander and Hughes argued inflation was as problematic to a social democratic economy as it was to a laissez-faire one. They suggested that wages be planned as part of an overall strategy including increased social spending and price controls. Such measures would ensure growth but were also linked, implicitly, to more radical interventions including public ownership. A national wages council would be founded to provide a forum to discuss settlements and to develop norms. Such an approach would, they claimed, offer a stable increase in real wages over time as well as helping to erode differentials and reduce sectionalism within the labour movement. It could also offer something more radical: Alexander and Hughes talked about pushing the limits of reform within capitalism.

As an attempt to generate wider public discussion on the issue the initiative was unsuccessful. There was virtually no press discussion of the pamphlet either in the general media (such as *The Guardian*) or in specifically trade union publications. However, a *Socialist Wages Plan* caused some controversy within the labour movement because after its election in 1964 the Labour government under Harold Wilson did implement an incomes policy as a central aspect of its economic strategy. Quite what relationship there might be between the two initiatives, though, is by no means obvious. Alexander and Hughes continued to lobby for the kind of programme they had put together in the pamphlet, most commonly in the pages of the *Tribune* newspaper. For the first few years of the Labour government they hoped that a radical version might emerge: 'for the past seven years we have been arguing that if the trade unions are to advance working class interests and extend social control over the economic system, they must develop coherent policies over the whole field of economic and social affairs, and that incomes policy is an issue around which this can best be done' (Alexander and Hughes, 1965, 6). They got some general support from surprising quarters. In notes on the subject, Ken Coates argued 'an increasing number of people are turning to the problem of details of the kind of plan upon which an incomes policy could be based ... It must be part of an overall strategy of advance towards social control of the economy' (1965, 5). Others, however, scholars and political campaigners alike, on the right as well as the left of the labour movement, were brutally critical of the Alexander-Hughes plan, arguing that it was economically flawed and would undermine the traditional roles and responsibilities of trade unions. Manifestly, it was an issue which did not command consensus across the left.

The New Left's grassroots

Lawrence Daly's enthusiastic endorsement of the wages plan, noted above, is interesting because he was a leading figure in the Fife Socialist League (see Thompson, 1978), the closest that the New Left came to developing a working class orientated political grassroots movements (one in marked contrast to its network of clubs). Having left the Communist Party in 1956, Daly was elected to Fife County Council in 1958 and stood against Labour in the 1959 general election with the enthusiastic support of John Saville and Edward Thompson, who campaigned for him and helped raised funds to finance his campaign. (Ken Alexander, based in Aberdeen, was resolutely opposed to Daly's interventions). Despite Daly's reference to Alexander and Hughes as 'a miner's Bible', the Fife Socialist League did not promote such a policy, making, as far as I can see, no direct reference to the subject. Of course, it may be unreasonable to expect such a relatively localised political body to develop a stance on national matters. However, the League did campaign heavily on a unilateralist platform. It received almost no coverage in the national press.

The New Left struggled to develop sustained support among active trade unionists. The publication of a specifically industrial bulletin followed a conference on the subject in early 1959 (Chun, 1993, 84). John Saville told Daly that he was 'more than ever persuaded that there are a lot of very good militants who can be brought into a loose grouping for general industrial and political meetings' (1959). A school discussing the wages policy was planned but it is not clear if it ever took place. A meeting in Manchester in September 1960 concluded that the development of some sort of network of the industrial wing of the New Left alongside the launch of an industrial journal was a priority. In Saville's words: 'The long term success of our work will depend on the quality of our thinking on industrial issues' (1959).

Just as the development of an organisational structure concerning economic and industrial issues proved difficult, so too, after the launch of *New Left Review*, did the articulation and publication of economic material in the journal. As editor, Stuart Hall mapped out an ambitious agenda on the subject for issues two, three and four. Hall pronounced: 'This debate is going to be a crucial one in the labour movement', yet noted that 'it is being conducted in the vaguest generalities' (Hall, 1960a). Few of the articles he proposed ever made it into print, though some of the alternative material that did come out, such as Charles Taylor's piece, did cover economic themes. It is interesting that Hall emphasised that he wanted a 'human dimension to the whole discussion' (1960b). At around the same time that Hall put together his proposals, another member of the editorial team told Lawrence Daly that they were having 'a hard time to find sufficiently solid material on the problems of this country' (Butt, no date). Later issues of the journal edited by Hall had even less economic material. By the summer of 1961, the New Left was struggling to sustain any momentum and most of its plans regarding economic and industrial matters fizzled out. A year or so later, as the first New Left came to an end, Thompson (1962) complained to Daly that it had 'failed even to form an industrial committee' (alongside other texts on this subject, see Hamilton, 2011).

Crosland's response to the New Left

In a 1962 published collection, Anthony Crosland directly targeted the New Left as *The Conservative Enemy*, albeit alongside the more obviously old-fashioned Old Left and the Conservative Party. He challenged Charles Taylor's notion that there were limits to the extent that profits might be taxed by the state, pointing out that other countries successfully set corporation taxes at a higher level. Look at Sweden, Crosland said: progressive taxation and welfare spending to promote equality have been combined with growth. Interestingly, Crosland criticised Richard Crossman for making much the same claim as had Taylor, though the former had written privately to Labour's chief revisionist on the subject after reading *The Future of Socialism* (see Wickham-Jones, 2007). The discussion of taxation is also significant given that Crosland seems to have modified his position in the early 1970s. By then, Stuart Holland had challenged the revisionist model, arguing that the state failed to tax monopolistic firms which under-reported and hid large profits. In *Socialism Now*, Crosland (1974, 29) responded by citing data deployed by Andrew Glyn and Bob Sutcliffe in their essentially neo-Ricardian account of the British economic crisis (a position developed along similar lines to that developed theoretically by Taylor). The share of profits in national product, Crosland claimed, had fallen as a result of state interventions.

In his most sustained assault on the New Left, Crosland devoted a chapter of *The Conservative Enemy* to taking on *The Insiders* and Barratt Brown's 'The Controllers'. For the most part, he argued, shareholders were weak, passive and ineffectual (with dispersed holdings). Part-time external directors with no expertise played no role. He continued to claim that power was dispersed throughout society. Any constraint owners offered to managers of a firm had to be balanced against the checks provided by the government, the trade unions, and public opinion. Crosland accused the New Left of 'a complete inability to understand who actually wields power in British society today' (Crosland, 1962, 81). He conceded that hostile takeovers raised issues but went on to suggest that 'such contests, for all the publicity which they attract, are comparatively rare' (Crosland, 1962, 68). There was effectively a convention prohibiting such initiatives: 'businessmen regard a proxy contest as an insolent, if not immoral, invasion of their management prerogatives' (Crosland, 1962, 68). By and large dividends reflected a 'conventional' level. They need not be maximised. Crosland asserted, 'An efficient company which generates a steady increase in earnings per share can pursue a conservative dividend policy and yet be invulnerable to takeovers; for asset values will not get out of line with share values' (Crosland, 1962, 84). In such circumstances, a sense of social responsibility was an important motivating factor for company managers.

Reviewing the volume, Barratt Brown restated the case made in *The Insiders* and 'The Controllers' about the class and elite identity of management in the United Kingdom. He argued that with competitive capital markets, firms needed to maximise profits. If they did not, share prices would be depressed and they would be a target for takeovers: 'If it is true that any company will be taken over unless it keeps up its profits, then the drive to maximise profits has to continue' (Barratt Brown, 1963, 27). Barratt Brown's proposition is one of the earliest statements on this subject from the left, though interestingly, in an article for *The Observer* in March 1962, Roy Jenkins linked ICI's hostile bid for Courtaulds to a dividend cut that had depressed the former's share price, making it a target for predatory takeover (Jenkins, 1962a). Jenkins argued that the dividend cut had been unnecessary on financial grounds. In successfully staving off the bid, Courtaulds responded by raising the interim dividend. Jenkins concluded that Courtaulds emerged from the battle 'committed up to the hilt to giving shareholders every penny that they could reasonably lay their hands on' (Jenkins, 1962b, 6). Crosland's claims about the character of British capitalism would, in retrospect, look to be at odds with arguments set out much later by Will Hutton (whose 1995 volume *The State We're In* covers similar ground to much of the analysis charted by the New Left). Hutton noted: 'On average, there have been 40 contested takeovers a year in London since the war; in Germany there have been four altogether' (Hutton, 1995b, 14). Add in the threat of a hostile takeover, and British firms do not appear to enjoy the kind of protection from predators that Crosland claimed for them.

Crosland did not engage with the kind of claims made by the New Left either about nationalisation or about wages policy. Moreover, the tone of the engagement was tetchy and bad-tempered. He cited the New Left's anger and inaccuracy: they were 'naïve and sloppy' (Crosland, 1962, 69). They displayed a 'masochistic inferiority complex' (Crosland, 1962, 81). Crossman, highlighting that phrase, accused Crosland of picking fights (Crossman, 1962, 24). In an interview in 1994 John Hughes suggested to me that the New Left 'didn't take Crosland's ideas seriously at all' and that 'there was no real reaction from Crosland': it was not an especially productive debate.

Conclusions

Taken together, the New Left, in its analysis of British capitalism's corporate and elitist nature; the case it made for nationalisation; and its articulation of a wages policy, offered a coherent social democratic model. On each of these issues they provided a significant challenge to Crosland's revisionism. Fifty years or so after the demise of the 'first' New Left, of course, the current policy relevance of its economic arguments are by no means straightforward, unsurprisingly given the changes undergone by the British economy as well as by society more generally. We can with care, however, derive some conclusions, both about the New Left's policies and, more broadly, about the way in which it articulated such arguments. Debates about the class structure and the networks underlying capitalism in the United Kingdom remain pertinent to reformism as do concerns about the structural nature of capital markets. By contrast, nationalisation no longer seems to be part of the social democratic agenda – other than in extremis – and, given the decentralisation of wage bargaining and decline of trade union membership, pay policy strategies no longer appear central to reformist economics. That said, issues of wage growth, competitiveness, and differentials do remain: by the late 1980s similar ideas to those floated by Alexander and Hughes had pretty much become part of social democratic orthodoxy, though their addition to the left-wing policy armoury owed little if anything to the New Left (see Wickham-Jones, 2013). Such measures were of course pursued in Sweden, while social pacts became an important institutional feature of some social democratic programmes elsewhere.

For all the apparent relevance of the New Left's economic material, such arguments did not have much impact on the broader labour movement. There are, I think, a number of reasons for this failure. Whilst the New Left developed a coherent challenge to Croslandite revisionism, arguably they were less effective in making such points public and generating debate. *The Insiders* received scant attention in the media. Reviewing Dennis Potter's volume *The Glittering Coffin*, Anthony Howard complained in *The Guardian* that 'the principal weakness of the New Left [was] – its tendency to conduct every one of its arguments and discussions within its own gold-fish bowl' (Howard, 1960). It is striking that nearly all of the reviews of Crosland's *The Conservative Enemy* do not even refer to, let alone discuss, his assault on the New Left. Barratt Brown, unsurprisingly, engaged directly with it. But most reviewers simply discussed the extent to which Crosland had revised the model mapped out in *The Future of Socialism*. The matters raised by the New Left were largely ignored.

The New Left failed to coordinate its arguments. It did not develop an overarching narrative that offered a wider perspective on economic matters, preferring for the most part to pick away at aspects of the revisionist model. It also failed to challenge the norms and conventions of the British labour movement. Both left and right objected to its wages policy on the grounds that it undermined the traditional role of trade unionists: in effect the plan came up against the norm of free collective bargaining to which the vast majority of the labour movement, Lawrence Daly notwithstanding, remained utterly committed. Space precludes a discussion as to whether the New Left might have paid more attention to such conventions and how it might have negotiated them. But, as an aside, it is worth noting that by the 1990s many leading trade unionists in the United Kingdom appeared less wedded to particular customs and informal rules, developing a more theoretical perspective on economic issues (I am thinking here, for example, of the discussions surrounding the development of a national economic assessment articulated by John Edmonds in the late 1980s and early 1990s).

As noted above, the New Left's relationship with the trade unions remained uncertain and undeveloped. There is a striking remark in Clive Jenkins' autobiography in this regard. In 1960 Jenkins launched *Trade Union Affairs*, a beautifully and stylishly produced journal by the standards of the day. Similar to *The New Reasoner* in format and aimed in part at an American market, it ran for around five numbers between 1960 and 1962. It might be expected that Jenkins, who had contributed to *The Insiders* and spoken at New Left meetings, would act as a contact point between the New Left and the unions. Yet the journal never offered any sort of engagement with the themes raised by the New Left, publishing just one article – by John Hughes on the rise of trade union militancy – from someone within its ranks. Jenkins is blunt: 'I did not want pieces by academics' (1990, 73).

When the first New Left came together once again as a political force in the late 1960s, with the May Day Manifesto, first in the form of a pamphlet, and subsequently in a Penguin special, it took care this time to offer a direct overall narrative about economic issues (Williams, 1968; see also Michael Rustin's article in this issue of *Renewal*). Edward Thompson (1967) told Daly that there was 'an overall connected analysis'. Interestingly, Ken Alexander and John Hughes did not contribute to the manifesto. Thompson's comments in this regard are telling. He acknowledged that 'it is of course weak in economic (esp. applied) areas, one reason being practical (the economists who offered help all let us down except for Michael BB [Barratt Brown] whose material was mainly on imperialism), the other theoretical – we found ourselves unable to accept the kind of gradualist policies advocated now by John Hughes (and Ken?)'. Thompson continued, 'That is with such a weak political movement and weak socialist consciousness, the old argument of *A Socialist Wages Plan* etc seems to me (at least for now) lost.' With the benefit of hindsight, it is by no means obvious that Thompson and his colleagues came up with anything to replace it.

Mark Wickham-Jones is Professor of Political Science at the University of Bristol.

An earlier version of this paper was given at the conference on 'The Labour Party and the British New Left' in June 2012: my thanks to the participants on that occasion, including Robin Archer and Paul Nowak, and the members of the Political Studies Association Labour Movements Group.

References

Alexander, K. and Hughes, J. (1959) *A Socialist Wages Plan*, London, Universities and Left Review/New Reasoner.

Alexander, K. and Hughes, J. (1965) 'Argument', *Tribune* 31.12.1965.

Barratt Brown, M. (1958, 1959) 'The controllers', parts I, II and III, *Universities and Left Review* 5, 6, 7: 53-61, 38-41, 43-9.

Barratt Brown, M. (1963) 'Crosland's enemy – a reply', *New Left Review* 19: 23-31.

Butt, D. (no date, but 1960) Letter to Lawrence Daly, MSS.302/3/3, Modern Records Centre, University of Warwick (MRC).

Chun, L. (1993) *The First New Left*, Edinburgh, Edinburgh University Press.

Coates, K. (1965) 'Incomes policy', mimeo, MSS 302/3/4, MRC.

Crosland, C. A. R. (1956) *The Future of Socialism*, London, Jonathan Cape.

Crosland, C. A. R. (1962) *The Conservative Enemy*, London, Jonathan Cape.

Crosland, C. A. R. (1974) *Socialism Now*, London, Jonathan Cape.

Crossman, R. (1962) 'Angry young men', *Guardian* 7.12.1962.

Daly, L. (1989) 'A miner's Bible', in Archer, R. et al. (eds.) *Out of Apathy*, London, Verso.

Davis, M. (2012) 'Arguing affluence', *Twentieth Century British History* 23 (4): 496-528.

Hall, S. et al. (1958) *The Insiders*, Universities and Left Review 3: i-iv and 25-64.

Hall, S. (1959) letter, *Guardian* 2.11.1959.

Hall, S. (1960a) Memo, 8.11.1960, MSS.302/3/3, MRC.

Hall, S. (1960b) Letter to Lawrence Daly, 8.11.1960, MSS.302/3/3, MRC.

Hamilton, S. (2011) *The Crisis of Theory*, Manchester, Manchester University Press.

Harrison, B. (1987) 'How the old train lost its way', *Guardian* 23.11.1987.

Howard, A. (1960) 'The lost tribes of the left', *Guardian* 2.8.1960.

Hughes, J. (1957) 'Steel nationalisation and political power', *New Reasoner* 2: 6-29.

Hughes, J. (1960) 'The commanding heights', *New Left Review* 21: 11-19.

Hutton, W. (1995a) *The State We're In*, London, Jonathan Cape.

Hutton, W. (1995b) 'How German-style institutions could help Britain to prosper', *Guardian* 16.1.1995.

Jenkins, C. (1958) 'Managerial revolution', notes, no date but talk on 17.3.1958, MSS 79/6/CJ/3/87, MRC.

Jenkins, C. (1990) *All Against the Collar*, London, Methuen.

Jenkins, R. (1962a) 'The thwarted giant', *Observer* 18.3.1962.

Jenkins, R. (1962b) 'How ICI became a thwarted giant', *Observer* 1.4.1962.

Kenny, M. (1995) *The First New Left*, London, Lawrence and Wishart.

Saville, J. (1959) Letter to Lawrence Daly, 16.7.1959, MSS 302/3/13, MRC.

Singh, A. (1975) 'Take-overs, economic natural selection and the theory of the firm', *Economic Journal* 85 (339): 497-515.

Taylor, C. (1960) 'What's wrong with capitalism', *New Left Review* 2: 5-11.

Thompson, E. P. (1962) Letter to Lawrence Daly, 29.9.1962, MSS 302/3/18, MRC.

Thompson, E. P. (1967) Letter to Lawrence Daly, 29.4.1962, MSS 302/3/4, MRC.

Thompson, W. (1978) 'The New Left in Scotland', in MacDougall, I. (ed.) *Essays in Scottish Labour History*, Edinburgh, John Donald.

Wickham-Jones, M. (1996) *Economic Strategy and the Labour Party*, Basingstoke, Palgrave.

Wickham-Jones, M. (2007) '*The Future of Socialism* and New Labour', *Political Quarterly* 78 (2): 224-40.

Wickham-Jones, M. (2013) 'The debate about wages', *The Journal of Political Ideologies* 18 (1): 83-105.

Williams, R. (ed.) (1968) *The May Day Manifesto 1968*, Harmondsworth, Penguin Books.

Lessons of the May Day Manifesto

Michael Rustin

This article discusses the political current which first defined itself as the New Left, and which emerged in Britain from the co-incident crises of the invasions (by Britain, France and Israel) of Suez, and by the Soviet Union of Hungary in 1956. This formation is sometimes referred to as the 'first New Left', since *New Left Review*, after 1962 when Perry Anderson succeeded Stuart Hall as its editor, developed a somewhat different intellectual and political project from that of the earlier journal and its *New Reasoner* and *Universities and Left Review* precursors (1).

Reflections on the recent past

This article focuses on the May Day Manifesto, which was published in May 1967, and in an expanded version as a Penguin Special in 1968 (2). It was first edited by Stuart Hall, Edward Thompson and Raymond Williams, each founding figures of the 'first New Left' of the mid-1950s. Various (then) younger people, such as Terry Eagleton and myself, contributed, in particular to the activities after the two launches, including the founding of May Day Manifesto groups in various towns, which followed, though on a smaller scale, the example of the New Left Clubs of the years prior to 1962. The Manifesto arose in part from a desire to maintain the active political engagements which had characterised the early New Left, and which its authors felt had diminished through the change in the orientation of *New Left Review*. The latter now adopted a more global perspective on prospects and strategies for the left, and was less concerned with local political involvements. But the Manifesto also arose from strong feelings of disappointment and disillusionment at what was happening to the Labour Government elected under Harold Wilson's leadership, in an atmosphere of promise, in 1964. The Manifesto was in part a critique of what it saw as the ongoing collapse of that government in the face of the pressures on it from international markets, from corporate capitalism, and from the continuing Cold War consensus.

Its main interest, looking at it now, lies in its argument that a holistic analysis of the then state of capitalism was necessary, and that without a grasp of the nature of the whole system and its interconnections, specific policies and reforms would fail. Indeed, it was held in 1967 that they were already failing. The 1964 Labour Government was already retreating from its own programme (for example for a National Plan) in the face of economic difficulties which culminated in the enforced sterling devaluation of November 1967.

Some of the themes of the Manifesto of 1967-68 remain current today. Its arguments citing the work of Peter Townsend on the persistence of poverty and inequality now have a renewed relevance. The critique of the excessive weight of the financial sector in the economy, and the weakness of British manufacturing – reflected in that pre-North Sea Oil era in chronic balance of payments problems – remain constants between these two periods. This argument was taken up most vigorously and effectively by Will Hutton (1995) in the intervening years, although the economic problems and imbalances have since become worse. Neo-imperialism also remains an issue throughout this entire epoch, with recurrent military interventions from the Falklands to the Iraq wars, Afghanistan, and Libya. The Manifesto writers were concerned with a growing divergence between single-issue, 'post-class' social movement campaigns, and a more traditional, Labourist 'working class' politics, and one of their main hopes was to see a reconnection of these 'new' and 'old' kinds of political movement. Its interest was in attempting to develop a unifying political narrative which took account of social and political diversification, while still remaining essentially socialist in its framing of the issues. One could say that its project was to show that new and old forms of oppression still had capitalism as their primary cause, while seeking to understand this as an evolving system, as a 'new capitalism'. The Manifesto's insistence on the necessity for a *socialist* frame of reference is a reminder of how the terms of debate have changed since 1967, and especially since the rise of New Labour in the 1990s.

In fact these different kinds of politics did soon become reconnected in reality after 1968 and through the 1970s, but in much more turbulent ways than the May Day Manifesto authors had anticipated. Both 'new' and 'old' forms of political action on the left became much more militant than they had been for years, with the industrial tensions of the 1970s, the anti-Vietnam War campaign, disturbances in the universities, and many other lines of emergent conflict, including those of gender and race.

These brought considerable social unrest during the 1970s, and indeed some saw in this unrest the spectre of 'ungovernability'. Ralph Miliband memorably described this as a 'state of desubordination' (Miliband, 1978). The 'corporatist' attempt to resolve these tensions during the 1960s and 1970s – via income policies, trade union reforms, indicative planning, social contracts and the like – failed, finally breaking down in the 'Winter of Discontent' of 1979. This had been essentially a last attempt to prolong and preserve the post-war class settlement. It was succeeded not by a renewed left – for which the Manifesto had argued – but instead by a renewed right, inspired and led by Mrs Thatcher. The Manifesto in 1967 and 1968 defined 'corporatism' and managerialism as its main adversary. In doing this, it anticipated some of the forms which the politics of modernisation would later take, not least under New Labour after 1997. It was a critique from the left of this emerging system, but did not recognise, as ten years later Stuart Hall and his colleagues did, that this unstable compromise would break down from its own contradictions, ushering in the era of Thatcherism (Hall et al., 1978). But the radical free-market ideology which underpinned the right in Britain from the late 1970s still remained relatively marginal in its influence in the 1960s, so it is not surprising that it was not identified as the Manifesto's main adversary.

From 1968, as the contradictions of the post-war consensus became evident, politics on the left became harder-edged in its texture than it had been in the early CND-dominated and somewhat utopian days of the early New Left, and this was also true on the political right. In terms of ideas, *New Left Review* and its publishing programme through Verso brought about a new theoreticism and a strongly Marxist inflection to political debate. This had significant benefits, in greatly expanding the intellectual resources available to socialists (and others), although at a cost of some separation of 'academic' from more everyday ways of thinking. One unexpected fruit of this theoretical development was the emergence of Charter 88, whose argument for a written constitution was influenced, through Anthony Barnett its leading animator, by the Anderson-Nairn thesis in *New Left Review* (1962; see also Michael Kenny's article in this issue of *Renewal*). Anderson and Nairn argued that Britain had failed to achieve a bourgeois revolution, which was in orthodox Marxism terms a necessary stage on the road to socialism. Trotskyists of various kinds became the dominant left tendency outside the Labour Party, and some Trotskyist factions pursued entryism within it. This political culture of neo-Leninism was a departure from that of the earlier New Left – it was, in fact, a regression – but it brought into being organisations with a greater tenacity and staying power than the New Left had been able to achieve, although CND had earlier created a substantial popular radical movement.

Both these theoretical and organisational developments had lasting legacies. A left intellectual culture developed, based in the expanding universities, but rather distant from locally-based political activity. Many of its adherents were more attentive to what was happening in Paris, as Edward Thompson (1965) acerbically observed, than to life in Leeds or Birmingham. This contrast between a flourishing left culture and a dominant right-wing politics was once memorably described by Perry Anderson as a 'culture in contraflow' (1990). The experiences of left penetration of the Labour Party brought, in reaction to it from the right in the 1980s, a determination to 'purge' the Labour Party of its radical elements, and of its broader democratic practices besides. My memory is that there had been closer links between Labour politicians – like Tony Crosland, Richard Crossman, Barbara Castle, Peter Shore et al. – and political intellectuals and academics on the left in the earlier days than has been the case since the 1980s. Sometimes these early links were formative for policy, as with the work on poverty and welfare of Richard Titmuss, Peter Townsend, and Brian Abel-Smith. Sometimes they took the form of ideological argument with New Leftists such as Raymond Williams, Edward Thompson, and Stuart Hall. Such links had been even stronger in the previous period of radical resurgence – see Paul Addison's *The Road to 1945* (1994) on the coming together of many radical and reforming currents in the making of Labour's 1945 programme. From the 1980s the Labour Party sought to become an ideology-free zone, with the GLC under Livingstone, and in some other Labour cities such as Sheffield, as exceptions (3). New Labour proclaimed that it wanted to leave behind ideologies, while itself of course constituting a new one, complete with its own theoreticians, not least Anthony Giddens, author of *The Third Way* (Giddens, 1998). Once New Labour took office in 1997, it firmly shut the door on the New Left intellectuals of *Marxism Today* (whose writing had not been without value for its development, not least in their critique of left fundamentalism), unless they were prepared wholly to identify with its project. There was little room under New Labour for constructive dissent.

Thinking about the present

Well, this was all a long time ago, so what has it and the New Left got to do with where we are now?

The most relevant contribution of this New Left tradition lies not only in its commitment to connected analysis of a 'whole system', but also and in particular to its interest in the nature of system crises or 'conjunctures', in Gramsci's terms. Stuart Hall and his colleagues (1978) analysed the crisis of the post-war class settlement, and of its last corporatist phase, during the late 1970s, in this theoretical frame. The power of its analysis of 'Thatcherism' arose from its understanding of the contradictions – the rising pressure of demands on capital and social hierarchy – to which the New Right offered a decisive political resolution. Hall (2003) analysed a later phase of this development, in his description of 'New Labour's Double Shuffle' as a politics which combined adaptation to a new world of globalised markets with its rhetorical self-presentation as the defender of popular interests and aspirations.

This tension between the pressures from organised capital and the need somehow to hold on to Labour votes brought New Labour's conspicuous addiction to politics as public relations – 'spin' – enthusiastically followed by Cameron, reportedly one of Blair's greatest admirers. Even though there were more tensions within the New Labour system than Stuart Hall was inclined to allow – for example the Brown–Blair battles were about real issues as well as personal ambitions – nevertheless the analysis of New Labour as essentially an adaptation to a neo-liberal world was correct.

But now we have the latest stage of this systemic development, which is the deep self-induced crisis of this entire system, following the near financial meltdown of 2007-8. The crisis of the 1970s had been the outcome of intensified class and other social conflicts, brought about through the strengthened position and demands of organised labour, arising from conditions of prosperity and full employment. This was a struggle over 'who governs?', over where social hegemony lies. But the financial crisis of 2007-8 was of a different order. This was an implosion of a financial system which had become decou-pled from the productive needs of the real economy. This was not a response to organised opposition to capital, since this had already been greatly weakened. As industries decamped overseas, and working and middle class living standards stagnated, resources were gambled in real estate markets and other forms of speculation. This is in part a crisis of under-consumption and insufficient economic demand, papered over by speculative borrowing and lending, in both public and private spheres, varying by nation. The with-drawal of government from economic planning and regulation has led in fact to greater economic weakness – the greater the deregulation, the greater the problems. (Where banks were more fully tied into long-term commitments to industries, as in Germany, or where government retained more economic responsibility, as in France, competitiveness was better retained). Particularly in the United States and in Spain, the banking crisis was fuelled by speculation in housing – through sub-prime mortgages in the USA – that insuffi-cient numbers of the population could afford to buy. Although welfare expenditures have to be kept in line with the capacity of an economy to pay for them in the long run, the reduc-tion of social protection, and of expenditures on such activities as health and education (themselves productive activities in their own right), will not restore the competitiveness of economies such as Britain's.

The New Left tradition's most relevant contribution in this crisis is its capacity to address the fundamental dysfunctionality of the system we now have, and the need to reflect on and map out the changes that are needed at a deep level. (*Soundings* has been developing this analysis in recent years: Davison and Rutherford, 2012). Just as the crisis of the 1960s and 1970s was a prolonged one, with successive governments failing in turn to resolve the UK's structural problems, so it seems possible that we are now in a crisis of a similarly extended kind. The main political risk may be less one of the Tories or the Coalition entrenching themselves in power, and more that Labour or a Labour-Liberal Democratic Coalition may win a General Election within two years or so, finding them-selves once again in government, but unable to act or even think outside the constraints of neo-liberal orthodoxies.

The short-term problems for Labour – maintaining a position in the polls, getting elected, avoiding a run on the pound, etc. – are real ones, and have to be recognised as such. But there needs to be a different kind of debate going on in parallel with tactical political and electoral concerns. What will this economic and political system have to become, if it is to be viable in twenty or thirty years time?

For example:

- What would a socially-accountable banking system look like, and how would it be owned and governed?

- How can the productive capacities of this society be described and mapped in such a way that an adequate 'industrial policy' becomes even conceivable? (One cannot have an industrial policy if one lacks even a map of the industrial and non-industrial productive economic sectors we have). This needs to be a model in which the activities of health provision, education, tourism, film and music-making, professional services of various kinds, for example, all count for as much as 'manufacturing', in the inventory of what is 'produced'. The traditional social democratic trade-off between a manufacturing and financial sector which is largely left to the 'free market' to generate wealth, and a public welfare system which is then enabled to consume part of its surplus, has to be abandoned. This is because on the one hand, the 'productive sectors' cannot in fact fend for themselves in a free market (most of Britain's remaining competitive economic sectors are already heavily dependent on their links with government, and a 'free market' hardly exists). And because on the other we have to think of health, welfare and housing systems as themselves generators as well as consumers of wealth.

- Inequality is an increasing problem, not only for reasons of ethics and comparative well-being, but also because if one prevents large numbers of people – obviously especially young people – from achieving their potential, in work and in other spheres, one depletes the capacities of the entire society. This should not be seen, as it conventionally is, as the goal of providing more opportunities for social mobility for selected talented individuals (for example expressed in a Prime Minister's rage at a talented state school pupil failing to gain entry to Oxford or Cambridge), but rather of ensuring that adequate opportunities and rewards are available for all. It is only in relatively equal societies that both 'upward and downward' mobility for individuals (one cannot, by definition, have one without the other) becomes possible.

- It is obvious that environmental constraints have to be taken as central to the future of British – and global – society, with 'well-being' and 'prosperity' redefined in ways that are consistent with a long-term, ecologically-sound future.

- The issue of democracy and democratisation is another fundamental dimension of 'the good and sustainable society' we should be thinking about. Here it is not just a question of constitutional adjustments (proportional representation, House of Lords reform, and the like), but of a conception of democracy that goes 'all the way down' into the governance of both public and private enterprises, and into the workplace. It needs to become a matter of teaching and learning democratic 'habits', of norms and practices of democratic leadership, as well as of laws and rules (Rustin and Armstrong, 2012). It seems likely that we will need to envisage parallel processes, both of the devolution of powers to local spheres of governance, and of their sharing and integration at a broader international level. The current process of a defensive and often chauvinistic default to restored national sovereignties seems likely to give rise to the worst of all worlds.

It seems to me important that a broader thinking and mapping process should be going on (as happened during the decade or so before the Labour Government of 1945 took office), which aims to influence and inform the immediate political process, without trying to take it over or become identical to it. This is why initiatives like 'Blue Labour' (whether or not one agree with its specific politics) are valuable.

Michael Rustin is Professor of Sociology at the University of East London.

A particular fragment of the New Left tradition by which I was formed is intending to publish a Soundings *Manifesto in monthly, free, on-line instalments, beginning in April 2013. It will be edited by Stuart Hall, Doreen Massey and myself, and may be subtitled, after two of our long-term places of residence, the Kilburn Manifesto. We intend that these arguments shall be further developed there. For further information go to http://www.soundings.org.uk/.*

References

Addison, P. (1994) *The Road to 1945*, London, Pimlico.

Anderson, P. (1990) 'A culture in contraflow', *New Left Review* 180: 41–78.

Anderson, P. and Nairn, T. (1962) 'Origins of the present crisis', *New Left Review* 23: 26-53.

Davison, S. and Rutherford, J. (eds.) (2012) *The Neoliberal Crisis*, London, Lawrence and Wishart, at http://www.lwbooks.co.uk/ebooks/NeoliberalCrisis.html.

Giddens, A. (1998) *The Third Way*, Cambridge, Polity.

Hall, S. (2003) 'New Labour's double-shuffle', *Soundings* 24: 10-24.

Hall. S., Critcher C., Jefferson T., Clarke, J. and Roberts, B. (1978) *Policing the Crisis: Mugging, the State and Law and Order*, London, Macmillan.

Hutton, W. (1995) *The State We're In*, London, Jonathan Cape.

Miliband, R. (1978) 'A state of de-subordination', *British Journal of Sociology* 29 (4): 399-409.

Rustin, M. J. and Armstrong, D. (2012) 'What happened to democratic leadership', *Soundings* 50: 59-71.

Thompson, E. P. (1965) 'The peculiarities of the English', *Socialist Register, 1965*: 311-62.

Notes

1. *The New Reasoner* existed from 1957 to 1959, *Universities and Left Review* from 1957 to 1959, and *New Left Review* was founded from the merger of the two in January 1960. The full texts of the two earlier journals are accessible at the Amiel-Melburn Trust Internet Archive: http://www.amielandmelburn.org.uk/archive_index.htm.
2. *Soundings* intends to republish the 1968 Manifesto, in May 2013, with a new Foreword. This will be available on-line at www.soundings.org.uk/.
3. A similar situation developed in Italy in the 1990s, where city mayors, such as Bassolino in Naples, Cacciari in Venice, and Rutelli in Rome, all elected to office in 1997, developed innovative forms of radical politics of which the former Communist Party of Italy, now the Democratic Party, was incapable in its national mode of operation.

Interview

Crises of capitalism and social democracy: John Bellamy Foster interviewed by Bill Blackwater

John Bellamy Foster is best-known as author of Marx's Ecology *(2000; in which he corrects the popular misapprehension that Marx did not 'get' environmental limits), and as editor of* Monthly Review *(http://monthlyreview.org/), the journal founded by Marxist economist Paul Sweezy in the late 1940s. In his latest book,* The Endless Crisis *(2012; written with Robert McChesney), Foster analyses what he calls the 'stagnation-financialisation trap'. This is the economic predicament countries such as the US and UK find themselves in today: dependent for growth on a system of financial bubbles which have now burst, they remain mired for the foreseeable future in a condition of chronic stagnation.*

Just as it used to be said of some people that they'd 'had a good war', so Foster and Monthly Review *have had a good financial crisis.* Monthly Review *had been predicting the crash, and the subsequent stagnation, for a long time. In the UK,* Monthly Review's *analysis has drawn favourable remarks from Larry Elliott of* The Guardian, *and its influence is on the rise.*

In this interview, John Bellamy Foster talks not just about the crisis mature capitalism finds itself in today, but the crisis this has wrought in social democracy. In many ways, for him this is the end of the line for social democracy: it can no longer hope to boost growth, and redistribute its spoils. Stagnation, not growth, is the order of the day. In these conditions, he argues, it is imperative that social democratic parties reinvent themselves, rebuilding links with their traditional sources of support, and crucial that they reinvigorate the political consciousness of the majority of the population who are being actively disadvantaged by the financial elites.

The stagnation-financialisation trap

In your new book, The Endless Crisis, *you and Robert McChesney talk about the 'stagnation-financialisation trap'. What do you mean by this?*

People commonly see what happened in 2007 and 2008 when the bubble burst as a financial crisis and nothing more. But the real problem is a tendency towards economic stagnation in the mature economies, and the long-term slowdown in the rate of growth.

Our argument is that financialisation, the series of financial bubbles that we've had over a period of decades, has been the main thing lifting the economy. I think this is fairly well understood now, but it wasn't understood so well five or six years ago. And while financial expansion has been lifting the economy, financial bubbles always have their limits. As the bubbles burst the government of course tries to act as the lender of last resort, pouring in liquidity and loans, to get the financial system going again. But it's not able to deal with the underlying problem which is stagnation, and this time we're stuck, they can't get the financial system really going again, and we're faced with a problem of economic stagnation that's surfaced as a result.

We call this the 'stagnation-financialisation trap' because the financialisation is the answer to stagnation but it creates bigger, more complex problems, and eventually the two problems together get us into a condition where we really can't move forward.

What are the roots of this condition of stagnation you're describing?

Basically, to understand the problem of stagnation, and also financialisation, you have to go back in time. We can go back as far as the Great Depression, which was a period of severe economic stagnation. And of course, we got out of the Great Depression mainly as a result of the Second World War, and after the War there was the period which we sometimes call 'the golden age' (although it had all sorts of problems itself), where the economy was going fairly well for all sorts of reasons. This had to do with the rebuilding of the European and Japanese economies after the War; basically the economy was very liquid because consumers hadn't been able to spend during the War, so there was a lot of purchasing power; there was the second wave of automobilisation; there was the Cold War which led to further military expansions. And all these things propelled the economy forward for a time.

But eventually, in the 1970s we ended up with a crisis and the economy started to slow down. In the 1970s the rate of growth was slower than in the 60s, it was slower in the 80s and 90s than the 70s, and it was slower in the first decade of this century than in the 1990s, and it looks like the economy is now slowing further. This was true of the United States; it's also true of Europe and Japan. So this is a problem of stagnation that's quite acute at this point.

Beginning in the late 1970s, for a few decades the economy was lifted by financial expansion, one financial bubble after another; the whole financial system grew relative to the underlying economy. Business elites couldn't find outlets for investment within what's called the real economy, or production, so they poured the economic surplus or savings at their disposal increasingly into financial speculation. That had the effect of lifting the economy in a secondary way, but then it eventually created bigger and bigger bubbles, bigger and bigger financial crises, and finally we come to one that the state as lender of last resort can barely handle at all, and we've got this interminable crisis. It's put us back into stagnation in a big way because we can't use financialisation effectively to expand the system, and there's no other way that anybody knows of, of how to expand the system on a long-term basis given the current conditions.

The limits of Minskyism

You mentioned earlier how the key role of financialisation in keeping the growth of the economy going has become only latterly more widely understood. Now, one of the key names in relation to that wider understanding more recently is Hyman Minsky. But I know that you part company with him, and I wonder if you could just spell out exactly where that is?

Starting in the 1960s, Hyman Minsky developed a theory of financial crisis. He came out of Keynes, and he was a socialist, but he focused on financial crises largely independent of what was going on in production – so he didn't look at the stagnation problem, or the underlying class dynamics much. He simply had a pure theory of financial crisis, where a financial system over time gets more and more unstable, because the more debt that's created, the quality of it diminishes, it becomes more speculative, and essentially you have a Ponzi system, and the whole financial structure threatens to come down, and the government has to come in as lender of last resort.

He didn't really deal with the relationship of this with the real economy, and he didn't deal with what we call financialisation, that is, the long-term trend in the growth of finance relative to production; instead he just focused on financial crises, one after the other, without looking so much at the long-term trend, the build-up of debt over decades. Only after the 1987 stock market crash, he wrote a piece for a book that I contributed to as well [Gottdiener and Komninos,1989], and he introduced a new notion of money-manager capitalism. He said, look, this is systemic now, we have an entire economic system that's dominated by money managers, who are basically running the show, and capitalism is fatally flawed. He was trying to work this out, but he didn't get very far.

Harry Magdoff and Paul Sweezy, meanwhile, in the 70s, 80s, and 90s, had written about the growth of financialisation as a response to stagnation in the underlying economy, and that's where I come out of.

Those who subscribe to the Minskyist view seem to argue that what we need to do is limit the role of the financial sector and then we can get back to 'good growth', and restore the primacy of the real economy. Now you're suggesting basically that this can't happen. This is presumably why you're calling this the 'endless crisis'? But in that case, how endless is it?

First of all, why can't the government and the central banks just regulate the financial system? Well, there's one main reason, and that's that you've got this underlying problem of economic stagnation. The expansion of the financial system, of the whole debt and credit apparatus, has been a way of utilising the economic surplus which isn't utilised in productive investment. It's instead poured into speculation, and that creates a wealth effect that has a secondary stimulus to the underlying economy, because as people who benefit from asset price increases get wealthier, they spend more on consumption, and that stimulates the economy. Finance also provides some jobs, although not as much as other sectors of the economy. So the financialisation of the economy has been this major stimulus, and it's helped keep the mature capitalist economies growing at a rate that's fairly low but considered adequate. And without the financialisation there's no real stimulus to growth. And this is the problem they have.

As a financial expansion slows, the authorities know they have a bubble. They know it's out of control. They know that the speculation's going to go so far, and that it will eventually burst. And what can the regulators do? They can try to clamp down on the speculation; but if they do, the bubble will burst, and the economy will go into crisis, and maybe into a very deep crisis and recession. Nobody wants that to happen on their watch. So they don't do it, they don't try to prick the bubble in advance. The government can't stabilise things under these circumstances because they're worried about pushing corporations that are 'too big to fail' over the edge; they're worried about the bubble bursting. The only thing they can do under these circumstances is give the investors more rope, and hope that when the bubble finally bursts, they're not the ones in office. And so this is the way the system works, it's not something that can be controlled in any rational sort of way.

In terms of the *Endless Crisis* [Foster and McChesney, 2012] – of course, nothing is really endless. Marx once referred, following Epicurus, to 'death the immortal'. In other words the only thing that is permanent is change, the passing away of existing conditions. But it does of course make sense to refer to an endless crisis in a more historically specific sense – in terms of the system itself and its current phase. The whole stagnation-financiali-sation trap is endemic to mature monopoly-finance capitalism. It might be that some new innovation will come along and save the day temporarily, but we've had the whole computer revolution, and it still hasn't stimulated investment adequately. Google might be seen as standing for such innovation. But it only employs some 20,000 workers in the entire United States, which is tiny. There's just no sign of anything on the horizon that will solve the demand-side problem of saturated markets and an increasing underemployment gap. The only solution of those in power, really, has been financialisation, and that in itself is very dangerous.

On top of all this we now have the additional problem that, because of the shift in accumulation from the industrial sector to the financial sector, we have a financial power elite that is basically running the show, which makes it doubly difficult to solve these things. Neo-liberalism is really a reflection of this shift towards a financialised system, or as I call it monopoly-finance capital.

The response to stagnation and recession in America and Britain

If we could turn now to the response to the crash and subsequent recession, in the UK over the last couple of years, people have pointed to the Obama Administration, and said that he has been responding to the recession in a much better way than the Conservative-Liberal Government here – that Obama has still maintained some stimulus spending and has achieved some growth as a result. What are your views about the way Obama has handled the recession?

When Obama came into office I wrote a piece with Robert McChesney called 'A new New Deal under Obama?' [Foster and McChesney, 2009]. But it was clear from the beginning that Obama would not offer much of an economic stimulus. And so there was a very small economic stimulus in the United States, $750 billion – that's over two years – and a very big part of it was tax reductions. The actual government spending increases that came out of it were meagre. So there really wasn't much of a direct government stimulus. I always imagine that when Obama was elected president the big boys at the Federal Reserve and the financial interests and Geithner brought him into the room and said: 'We'll let you have your little stimulus, but we're going to put more than $10 trillion into bailing out the financial system and that's where the real game is, and yours is just for show.' I'm just making this up of course, no one has any way of knowing how this played out behind closed doors in the White House, but it was sort of like that. What was done in terms of fiscal policy was meagre compared to what was done through the Federal Reserve and monetary policy, essentially printing money.

The US economy is not doing very well – it's stagnating, the big issue is economic stagnation, because unemployment is enormously high – especially if you look at the U6 instead of the U3 figures (the real unemployment, which takes into account the effects on labour participation and so on). Unemployment and underemployment by the U6 figure is currently over 14 per cent.

In Britain, of course, you've had a double-dip recession, and are worried about a triple-dip. This has to do in part with the fact that Britain has gone much further in adopting austerity programmes that go against everything that we know about economics and what you do in a recession. The country that produced John Maynard Keynes seems to be totally ignorant of fiscal policy and strategy – but it's more than that – it's not simply a question of bad policy. In Britain, as I understand it, the City is much more central even than Wall Street is in the United States. Basically, the British system is more dependent on financial power than is the United States. Under these circumstances the authorities are doing what the financial interests want – which isn't necessarily what's good for production or for the economy or for employment or income. But it does help those with money. Those with money capital – especially the big financial interests, the banks, insurance companies, hedge funds – are primarily concerned about one thing right now, and that's preserving their capital. We're in a period where maintaining the value of existing financial assets is actually the number one issue, and this is clearly driving British policy, and to a lesser extent that of the United States.

Monthly Review's influence

Can I ask about the influence now of your ideas, and of Monthly Review *more generally? To what extent has the financial crisis given* Monthly Review *wider influence in the mainstream media?*

Well, we struggle. *Monthly Review* has, I think, a growing influence on the left in the United States and worldwide, among those willing to listen, but in the mainstream US media – which means the corporate media – we've made very little in the way of inroads at all. The media is conservative by any standard, and it's very corporate-controlled. Indeed, the media are themselves giant, monopolistic corporations. Hence, we represent a viewpoint that's off-limits. Although certain business and financial interests follow us closely, it is certainly not something that normally comes out into the open too often. We do, however, have an impact within the left and the movement in general, and also among political economists and heterodox economists – and I think all of this is growing.

What is interesting today, and I would certainly not attribute it to our direct impact at all, is that some prominent liberal economists are gradually moving under the force of events toward an assessment that reflects where we've been all along. Paul Krugman in recent years has rediscovered stagnation, and after the financial crisis he started reading Minsky, followed by Kalecki. Now in the last few months or so he's discovered monopoly power and labour versus capital – he says he never realised that labour-saving innovations could be so destructive to labour. And he says that he's basically discovering the value of an old-fashioned Marxist sort of view! Of course this doesn't mean he is about to become a radical; only that he is forced to approach the economy these days with a greater degree of realism.

The issues that we've been talking about in *Monthly Review* are more and more central to current conditions, and so we have an impact on the discussions taking place amongst informed individuals in the financial community as well as left intellectuals. But in the United States the political climate is still very different to that in Britain. In the UK, the fact that a Labour leader had a Marxist father might not actually destroy his political future in Parliament, but in the United States the right-wing is very powerful. They're constantly trying in the mass media to link Obama to the left, and to demonstrate that he's a 'socialist', which of course is a patent absurdity. There's still this kind of mini-McCarthyism that's never really gone away. The 'respectable left' itself frequently gives into this, policing itself to be as liberal-sounding as possible, and to downplay any lingering socialism in words as well as deeds.

What about on university campuses in North America? I'm wondering to what extent the younger generation is exposed to and seeking out your kind of arguments?

Well, I personally have more invitations to speak on campuses than I can possibly ever fulfil, they're just growing massively. I do a few and I try to farm out talks to others. *Monthly Review* is now known for three things – it's known for its analysis of the ecological crisis and for its understanding of monopoly capitalism, stagnation, financialisation, and the whole economic trap that we're in. Plus there is the third area, that goes way back, of the critique of imperialism.

There's a lot of people who are calling on us for the environmental analysis, and have been for some time; and now there's more and more people who are focusing on the economic failures of capitalism. It's the youngest (and perhaps the oldest) activists today who are mostly focusing on the economy; whereas, let's say those in their thirties and forties on the left have been concerned more with the environment. It's a strange situation. Because a while ago, the economy wasn't so much the issue, while the environment was; now it's the economy, but especially among younger people, people who were influenced by the Occupy movement.

The end of capitalism?

The bigger question hanging over all this, going back to what you said about how of course nothing is really endless, is: how do you see things playing out? And is this the end of growth? And does that mean it's the end of capitalism?

There are old theories of economic breakdown (where Henryk Grossman is the most famous example) that still have some currency among the left – the notion that the system will just economically break down due to a falling rate of profit, and in the midst of it the left will rise. But capitalism isn't going to exactly economically break down: what we have is a problem of stagnation, which is very slow growth and rising unemployment (and underemployment) and excess capacity. So the system doesn't really collapse, but because the pie is not increasing, in order for capital to get its profits and accumulation, they have to take bigger slices of the pie, which means everybody else gets smaller slices, so inequality increases. The system just sort of splutters along, and the conflicts get more intense, but there's no actual economic breakdown. Gar Alperovitz is calling the economic situation one of 'punctuated stagnation', that is slow growth, punctuated with deeper economic setbacks, maybe due to bubble-bursting events. What we need is for people to realise how disastrous this system is, and especially those on the bottom who are really losing out – they have to organise, and begin to create something quite different.

The ecological crisis of course makes this even more pressing. We have just a few decades at most in which to solve that problem, or we lose control of climate change, and the ability to prevent the world reaching a planetary tipping point. We're looking at the possibility that if we reach 2-degrees Celsius we are facing extremely dangerous climate change with all sorts of feedbacks so that things will likely be beyond our ability to control.

Economically and environmentally we don't really have a lot of latitude now. We have a system that's economically performing very poorly, and becoming more unequal all the time, it relies on a global labour arbitrage that exploits people in the global South at horrendous rates, it's destroying the planet as a place for human habitation. We're facing overlapping material crises and we can't think simply in economic terms any more.

Just to clarify what you were saying there, you don't see a classic breakdown of the capitalist system in terms of pure economics, but you do see a genuine potential for a fundamentally different economic system to actually replace it?

The potential is there, of course. In the United States, almost everything that we produce is a form of waste. There's very little that we produce that is actually useful to human beings; very, very small percentages of production have to do with genuine use values. And we have the potential to reorganise the economy to meet people's needs and to decrease all of this waste, but we have to decide to do it. We spend a trillion dollars a year, conservatively speaking, in the United States on marketing, just every year convincing people to buy things that they don't really want. And what we produce as a result of that is mostly waste as well. Consequently, we have the means to improve people's lives with the resources we have, and while even shrinking the economy.

We have the capacity to solve these problems, but only if we are willing to change our social relations fundamentally. It's also an actual necessity – since if we continue the way we are for much longer, in ecological terms we'll go over the cliff. In economic terms people aren't doing very well either. We just simply need a different kind of society, and we have to try to build it; there's no blueprint.

And this would not be a society based on continuous economic growth?

That's right, it can't be a system geared to exponential economic growth. You know, the word growth is so distorted now that people think it is primarily an economic term. But in classical economics they didn't even use the term 'growth'. And of course everybody believes in growth, that's why it's such a nice metaphor – but growing what? What we measure as economic growth in today's society is often negative – we should be subtracting what we're actually adding. For example, if there is an oil spill we end up adding to, not subtracting from, GDP. All the clean-up costs and litigation costs increase GDP. There is no subtraction, though, for environmental losses, welfare losses, or anything else. And this is a large part of the problem. We consider it growth so long as something passes through the market, whatever it is. And inversely those things that don't pass through the market (such as the sea turtles that are rapidly being driven into extinction) have no value. Their loss is simply an 'externality' – of no real significance to the economy or growth. But we can't afford to approach things this way anymore – because that means a system that's only interested in one thing, and that's production of profits at the top, regardless of what we're actually producing or the damage we are inflicting on the planet and global society. We can't afford such a crude perspective in a world that is so limited, where there are real planetary constraints. Moreover, despite their emphasis on abstract economic 'growth' those at the top can't even promise to the population a 'trickle down' any more. There are no real economic benefits for the majority of the people from today's pattern of accumulation. All we can do under this system geared to endless accumulation of capital is to destroy the environment and our lives.

What this means for social democracy

Social democracy has sought to work within the capitalist system but to redistribute its fruits more equally, and indeed to make it work more efficiently. So where does the current crisis of capitalism leave social democracy and parties such as Labour?

Well, I think social democracy in the traditional sense is really in an impossible situation now. For one, the idea was to promote growth and redistribute it, but there is no way to definitely promote growth. You could have a Keynesian-style expansion for a short while, and it would probably be a good thing to do given the present crisis. But the problem is that we have a highly financialised, not to speak of globalised, system now, so we really have a system that's dominated by monopoly-finance capitalism – and the old Keynesian strategy doesn't work in that context, because that strategy goes against the financial interests which really dominate the system. Keynes argued for the euthanasia of the rentier. Today's rentiers have demanded the euthanasia of Keynesianism. There's no other way to expand the system at present that is acceptable to the financial power elite but by promoting financialisation, which also increases the power of the financial power elite.

In the United States, we of course still rely heavily on military spending, we have a history of military Keynesianism – you do too. The United States in reality spends a trillion dollars on military spending. We do this rather than promoting civilian government spending. Even by the official figures the United States spends as much on the military as all the other countries of the world put together, but this isn't enough of a stimulus anymore.

Social democratic policies are predicated on a growth that doesn't exist anymore. They are predicated on an industrial capitalism that doesn't exist anymore, or not in the same sense. And they are predicated on a more national than globalised system. So it's very hard to promote any kind of social democratic policy now. Social democratic politics always had its contradictions because of its compromise with capitalism, which was prob- lematic from the start. Capital always maintained overall social power. But today things are more complicated. We are now in a phase not so much of monopoly capital, during which labour and capital were able to negotiate to a degree, as monopoly-finance capital, where labour is pushed to the wall. Financial interests are a much stronger part of the whole; the industrial sector, particularly labour, is weaker; and production is increasingly globalised. I think you could probably reinvent social democracy. But it would have to be a movement that turned back to the people and mobilised the population in new ways, marking radical changes fundamentally opposed to what social democracy has traditionally stood for. It would have to, in other words, become more not less socialist. It also has to be part of a more international strategy, involving international labour alliances. Social democracy grew out of the socialist movement, now it has to return to the genuine socialism it abandoned. Of course another way of saying this is: social democracy is dead, long live socialism.

You were a friend of Ralph Miliband's. What advice do you think he would want to give to Ed Miliband today?

That's a difficult question! I didn't know Ralph really well, I met him a number of times, but I was so junior to him that it was not really on anything like an equal basis. He encouraged me. I wrote for the *Socialist Register* when he was editor. And I remember him as the harshest editor (in a good sense) I ever confronted. He was really a serious scholar. He was strong on rooting out non sequiturs. I wrote a piece on liberal practicality and the US left, based on C. Wright Mills, and Mills' notion of vocabulary of motive and crackpot realism [Foster, 1990]. The argument was that, if the left continually adopted liberal discourse or vocabularies of motive and liberal ways of thinking in order to try to present its ideas, eventually it would lose its grasp on reality, and its ability to respond to the population. I had all sorts of examples like the common use on the left of the notion of a 'social contract' between capital and labour, which hardly existed in fact. Ralph liked my argument.

I think the left has been faced with this issue of liberal practicality for a long time, watering down its ideas to conform to the dominant view to the point that it is no longer able to develop a strategic orientation. There has been a long attrition with respect to critical ideas, and a kind of long march back towards liberalism. Today the social democrats are basically in the position of the capital 'L' Liberals of old, and they've lost sight of the more radical views and the links to unions and workers and so on that were so vital to their origins. Somehow they have to get back to that, to those roots, but to do it in a new way.

Ralph was famous of course for the debates on the state. He used to argue in works like *The State in Capitalist Society* that the relative autonomy of the capitalist state from the capitalist class or the plutocracy in today's world wasn't very great, which meant a much stiffer social struggle. Others like Nicos Poulantzas (with whom he was chiefly in dispute) argued that there was much more relative autonomy, and that you could have a euro-socialist or euro-communist movement, which if it managed to get itself into office could effectively change things within the existing rules. It seems to me that in terms of this debate Ed Miliband is closer to Poulantzas' way of thinking than to that of his father – or that has been his attitude so far. Labour in reality can only move forward in one way, and that's by enlisting the population as a force in society, mobilising them in terms of a new social project – exactly what Ed Miliband's father would have recommended. In other words, what relative autonomy there is for the state to foster social change within capitalism requires a huge social/class struggle on an extra-parliamentary even more than parliamentary basis and the creation of an entirely new social project. This has always been the conundrum of what Ralph called 'parliamentary socialism'. (Incidentally, Monthly Review Press published Ralph's book by that title in the United States).

Would you say that there is a previous period of debate on the left which contemporary social democrats could go back to and reread, in terms of trying to rediscover something to relaunch social democracy as you're describing it here?

The debates within the British left in this area were at one time very meaningful, the debates around parliamentary democracy, the debates around the state. All of this has been forgotten. I would suggest reading those who were classified like Ralph Miliband as instrumentalist theorists – theorists who believed that the state at present was primarily the instrument of the capitalist class. We need this deeper understanding to develop a sophisticated state-society strategy that addresses capital's social power. The most powerful strategic version of change ever presented to the British Labour Party I think was that of Michał Kalecki in his 1942 essay on 'The essentials for democratic planning', which was written for *Labour Discussion Notes* [reprinted in Kalecki, 1986]. I have written about that in an upcoming article in *Monthly Review* [Foster, 2013]. The situation has changed but Kalecki's understanding of political-economic strategy is still invaluable.

The question is: how do you enlist the population as a force, how do you reinvigorate people, give them a social project that's being developed from the ground up, that will enlist their support? Look at Venezuela – obviously the situation is very different, but they're very good at enlisting the mass support of the population by social projects at the ground level, giving them the sense that they can do something to change their own society. If you don't do that, you can't possibly have any force for political change on the left.

My final question continues my interest here in social democracy and its past record – one of the things I'm particularly interested in is the contrast between Monopoly Capital, *as in the book Paul Sweezy and Paul Baran wrote [1968], and* Supercapitalism, *the 2007 book by Robert Reich. Reich describes the post-war period as the 'not quite golden age', and makes the case that it was actually monopoly capitalism which enabled giant corporations, who felt insulated from competition, to do deals with unions which delivered greater shares of wealth to working people. I wondered what you thought about that argument, and what, if any, relevance does it have for today?*

Robert Reich is very smart and genuinely concerned about labour. But his argument as a whole, as I understand it, strikes me as wrong. It's based on the notion that's very common in liberal circles that somehow we could get back to the 'golden age' (or as he calls it 'not so golden age'), and that this was based on some kind of corporatism, or what he calls 'democratic capitalism', where large firms and large labour got together. In this view, Fordism was promoted, there was a social contract, and so on and so on. I think it's just fundamentally a wrong reading of history. The post-Second World War prosperity was a very special historical result, coming out of the War, McCarthyism, the Cold War, etc. To view the period as the triumph of democratic capitalism, which we have to somehow recapture, is to misread, I think, both the past, and even more what is possible in the present. It is true that monopoly capital had a very limited accord with big labour in the context of the Cold War, militarism, imperialism, the struggle with the Soviet Union, the destruction of the radical unions, etc. But this was a complex history. It was also a period that led straight down the path to the decisive defeat of labour in the United States. There is no possibility of a new democratic capitalism or corporatism today in a context where only some 11 per cent of workers are organised, and most of those are in the state sector; where 14.4 per cent of the real labour force wants but cannot get a full-time job; and where labour's power within the state has receded to almost nothing. Reich is no doubt correct to say that we live in a more vicious world of capitalism (as far as US workers themselves are concerned) than in the 1950s and 60s. However, it is not some sort of supercapitalism (or neo-liberalism) that is the problem, nor the displacement of democratic capitalism. Rather the problem lies with capitalism itself, which has necessarily evolved in this direction. Moreover, it is not a world of unrestrained competition but of greater global, monopolistic control in a highly financialised, globalised system.

The revenues of the top 200 US corporations account for more than 30 per cent of all gross profits in the U.S. economy, and there are millions of firms in the economy, so you have a very highly concentrated system. But labour has shrunk almost into non-existence. It certainly would be great to rebuild the labour movement, but you're going to have fight corporate capital all along the way, there's not going to be any corporatist solution. Socialism is the only answer. But there is no royal road to genuine socialism. It requires what Raymond Williams [1961] used to call a 'long revolution'.

John Bellamy Foster is Professor of Sociology at the University of Oregon and Editor of *Monthly Review*.

Bill Blackwater is an Associate Editor of *Renewal*.

References

Baran, P. A. and Sweezy, P. M. (1968) *Monopoly Capital: An Essay on the American Economic and Social Order*, Harmondsworth, Pelican.

Foster, J. B. (1990) 'Liberal practicality and the US left', *Socialist Register* 26: 265-89.

Foster, J. B. (2000) *Marx's Ecology: Materialism and Nature*, New York, Monthly Review Press.

Foster, J. B. (2013) 'Marx, Kalecki and socialist strategy', *Monthly Review* 64 (11), at
http://monthlyreview.org/2013/04/01/marx-kalecki-and-socialist-strategy.

Foster, J. B. and McChesney, R. W. (2009) 'A new New Deal under Obama?', *Monthly Review* 60
(9), at http://monthlyreview.org/2009/02/01/a-new-new-deal-under-obama.

Foster, J. B. and McChesney, R. W. (2012) *Endless Crisis: How Monopoly-Finance Capital
Produces Stagnation and Upheaval from the USA to China*, New York, Monthly Review
Press.

Gottdiener, M. and Komninos, N. (eds.) (1989) *Capitalist Development and Crisis Theory*, New
York, St Martin's Press.

Kalecki, M. (1986) *Selected Essays on Economic Planning*, Cambridge, Cambridge University
Press.

Miliband, R. (1964) *Parliamentary Socialism*, New York, Monthly Review Press.

Miliband, R. (1969) *The State in Capitalist Society*, New York, Basic Books.

Reich, R. (2009 [2007]) *Supercapitalism: The Battle for Democracy in an Age of Big Business*,
London, Icon.

Williams, R. (1961) *The Long Revolution*, Harmondsworth, Penguin.

Leveson uncut

Leveson, politicians and the press: origins of the present crisis

Helena See

The storm surrounding the Leveson Inquiry into the culture, practices and ethics of the press has been brewing for at least 30 years. This is certainly not the first time society has collectively revulsed against the ethics of the popular press. As Lord Justice Leveson has himself remarked, it is only 'the latest in a long sequence of spikes in public concern about press standards' (Leveson, 2012b, 25).

The history of the twentieth century is littered with attempts to strengthen press regulation – including three Royal Commissions in 1947, 1962 and 1974, the Younger Commission of 1972, and the two Calcutt Reviews of 1990 and 1993. The Leveson Inquiry is the seventh such attempt in less than 70 years. Yet every British government to date – many of whom were responding to reports that they themselves had commissioned – has failed to put in place anything more stringent than variations on the theme of self-regulation. This article gives one account of why this has been the case, and why we are unlikely to see a departure from form in our present situation.

The remit of the Leveson Inquiry is extremely broad, taking in the relationship of the press with the public, with politicians, and with the police; commercial issues like press concentration; and the future of press regulation. Yet only one of these strands – the relationship between politicians and the press – may ultimately hold the key to all the rest.

This article locates the genesis of a new kind of relationship between government and press with the extraordinary intimacy Margaret Thatcher cultivated with the tabloids during her term in office. In 1979, the year she came to power, *The Sun* was described by *The Observer* as 'Mrs Thatcher's missionary outpost to the working-class voter' (6.5.1979). By the time she left office a decade later, *The Sunday Telegraph* was willing to accept that, 'the support of *The Sun* can make or break the fortunes of the Tory Party' (24.6.1990).

Every subsequent Prime Minister, whether Conservative or Labour, has had to come to terms with this doubled-edged aspect of Thatcher's legacy. Thatcher's relationship with the tabloid press was a powerful weapon for any successor to inherit – but as the scandal-driven collapse of the Major administration vividly demonstrated, it came with a dangerous degree of vulnerability to an ever-mightier media empire.

Together, Thatcher and Major set a double precedent for New Labour in 1997. Whilst Thatcher demonstrated the rich rewards to be reaped from the relationship she constructed with the popular press, Major's fall illustrated the devastating consequences of disregarding its rules. Against the backdrop of this cautionary tale, it is hardly surprising that subsequent leaders of both left and right have come to accept the terms of this power relationship as a fundamental premise of British political culture.

Backlash: how the sixties set the scene

The relationship between Thatcher and the tabloid press was authentic in a way that none of her successors – not even Blair – were ever able to emulate. In part, this is because their affinity was not the conscious product of any official mechanism, but stemmed from the immediate social and cultural context of previous decades.

Britain in the 1980s was a society ill at ease with itself. Despite the much-heralded 'revolution' in social attitudes that came with the 1960s, the vast majority of the British public regarded the sexual liberation movements and 'permissive' reforms of that era as the work of a remote political and intellectual elite. As one *Sun* editorial put it as late as 1994: 'It doesn't bother MPs that a consistent 75% of the British people want vicious killers to be hanged. It doesn't impress them that most of us feel deeply uneasy at condoning acts of teenage homosexuality. *Parliamentarians prefer to rely on their own consciences*' (12.1.1994, emphasis in original). Evidence from the British Social Attitudes survey shows that the proportion of respondents who believed homosexual relations to be 'wrong' actually rose to 74 per cent in 1987, up from 62 per cent in 1983. Similarly, the proportion of respondents who believed extra-marital sexual rela-tions to be 'wrong' rose to 88 per cent in 1987, up from 83 per cent in 1983 (Smith, 1994, 51).

Recent contributions in the field of media and cultural studies have demonstrated the important function that popular journalism plays in 'cultural reinforcement'. As a form of ritual communication, it allows us to consolidate a shared identity, and to 'rehearse our moral sensibilities' through the constant iterations of repetitive journalistic tropes (Gripsrud, 2004). For the tabloids, the uneasy cultural inheritance of the 1960s opened up a market for stories and tropes which served to bolster and reinforce the 'traditional' values that were perceived to be under threat. For Thatcher, popular unease about permissiveness presented an opportunity for her to position herself as the voice of the common man, speaking out against those intellectual elites who had imposed permissive reform on the population against its will.

Like the reassuring rhetoric of the tabloid press, Thatcherite policy deftly channelled popular suspicion of these elites and the permissive values they condoned. Section 28 famously banned the 'promotion' of homosexuality in schools as a 'pretended family rela-tionship', in stark contrast to the sexual normalcy and nuclear family structures that would restore the nation to moral health. It managed to present homosexuality as a kind of Politically Transmitted Disease carried by the 'loony left', and by so doing, imbued the moral backlash against the gay rights movement with a sense of national urgency.

Perhaps the most ingenious of all Tory constructs, the 'loony left' furnished the tabloids with a rich and never-ending seam of entertaining stories: in the mid-1980s it was reported that Labour-controlled local authorities had banned the nursery rhyme 'Baa baa black sheep' and black dustbin liners as racist (Thomas, 2005, 94). Moreover, in its repetitive and unrelenting association of the left with unpopular permissive causes, this tabloid trope carried the Conservative message beyond the traditional Tory heartlands, and into the new, remoter electoral provinces of the Murdoch empire. At the 1994 local elections, *The Sun* was still officially endorsing the Conservatives against Labour councils who 'hand out YOUR cash to barmy politically correct causes like lesbian and gay clubs' (4.5.1994). Arguably, the strength and insistence of this association did more to advance the Conservatives' party-political strategy than their own pronouncements on such matters.

The political capital of moral panics

Later Tory leaders have all played to these resonances in one way or another – and in this they have been joined by many Labour leaders too. Conservative politicians in particular have a habit of lapsing into moral hyperbole when there is political capital to be gained from a wider sense of social anxiety. Upbraiding a 'broken' society and urging national regeneration through stronger family life has proven to be an effective – and cheap – way to reap mass support at times of social unease or moral panic.

Just as Thatcher responded to popular anxiety about permissive reform, David Cameron built his 2010 election campaign (with the help of *The Sun*) around the motif of 'Broken Britain', and John Major produced his ill-fated 'Back to Basics' campaign in the wake of Black Wednesday and the murder of James Bulger. Indeed, some historians have gone so far as to argue that 'Back to Basics' was 'the political and ideological reaction to the Bulger case' (Franklin and Petley, 1996, 149). Whilst this is probably an overstatement of the importance of the Bulger incident relative to other imperatives like Black Wednesday, it highlights the ease with which a single symbolic event can be exploited for political gain. More specifically, it demonstrates how the presentation of such an incident as indicative of social, moral, and familial decay can be an expedient and unifying strategy when faced with challenging political conditions and unpopular policy decisions.

This strategy was explicitly acknowledged by Tony Blair in a fascinating article for *The Guardian* written shortly after the riots of August 2011. Reflecting on the similarities between the public reaction to the riots and the public reaction to the Bulger case, he condemned those who 'elevated' the riots 'into a high-faluting wail about a Britain that has lost its way morally', before admitting that, 'In 1993, following James Bulger's murder, I made a case in very similar terms to the one being heard today about moral breakdown in Britain. I now believe that speech was good politics but bad policy' (*Guardian*, 20.8.2011).

Major's fall: the exception that proved the rule

Though subsequent leaders have all shown themselves willing to capitalise on the political benefits facilitated by Thatcher's media revolution, some have been less willing to recognise the higher expectations that came with the new status quo.

Thatcher created a political culture in which the personal was political and the political was personal. This was something that Major was prepared to accept whilst extolling 'those old, commonsense British values that should never have been pushed aside' (Major, 1993), but took on quite a different complexion in the midst of the notorious string of sexual and financial scandals that plagued nearly a dozen Conservative ministers and MPs during the 1990s. By trying to claim that the personal lives of erring ministers like David Mellor and Tim Yeo were 'purely private matters', Major refused to acknowledge the extent to which years of stories by these very tabloids on 'private matters' like sexual morality had served to bolster his party's standing with the electorate. To Major, 'Back to Basics' may well have been a cynical communications exercise – but for the press, it was deeply intertwined with one of the defining news agendas of the era.

This disparity underlines a key dimension of what went wrong for Major – rhetoric which he deployed, sometimes successfully, for short-term political gain, was amplified by the much more insidious moral tropes which continued to embed themselves in the popular press. The very discourse that had thrived to the Conservatives' advantage in the populist political climate of the 1980s and early 1990s ultimately proved to be the instrument of the Major government's destruction.

As is well known, the disintegration of the Conservative-Murdoch alliance under Major was swift and brutal. The devastating effectiveness with which the tabloid press dismantled Major's hopes of re-election in 1997 revealed the unassailable position of strength to which it had ascended during the Thatcher years. Though sleaze was not the only issue at stake in Major's twilight hours, it was the means by which the tabloids were able to control the news agenda and drown out any attempt by the government to regain the political initiative. *The Sun's* headline on Black Wednesday, 'Now we've ALL been screwed by the Cabinet' (17.9.1992), is a brilliant example of the way in which it kept sleaze at the forefront of political consciousness. By keeping the issue of sleaze perpetually in the public eye, the tabloid press made it impossible for the Conservatives to make a lasting and positive political impact on any other issue.

Major's landslide defeat in 1997 was a cautionary tale for future leaders on the perils of estranging the Murdoch empire. As the later efforts of Blair, Brown and Cameron to curry favour with News International have shown, Major was the last Prime Minister to fail to appreciate the power of Murdoch and the tabloid press. After his example, no leader would make that mistake again.

'One last chance' for self-regulation

Such pragmatism on the part of party leaderships has not, however, tended to penetrate the party ranks. Parliamentary debate on statutory regulation of the press has always been lively, but within this wider tradition there has been a continuous body of cross-party support for stiffer regulation. The 1980s saw a steady stream of Private Members' Bills from both sides of the House proposing greater protections for victims of press intrusion. This was bolstered by a rising tide of anti-press sentiment in the public at large, provoked in particular by a series of high-profile stories involving members of the royal family. Andrew Morton's biography of the Princess of Wales, which was serialised in *The Sunday Times* in June 1992, revealed to the public her struggle with bulimia and depression, her suicide attempts, and the relationship between the Prince of Wales and Camilla Parker-Bowles. This was swiftly followed by *The Sun's* publication of transcripts of a bugged telephone conversation between Diana and her friend James Gilbey known as the 'Squidgy tapes'. In the same month, *The Daily Mirror* published photographs of the Duchess of York sunbathing topless with the American financial adviser John Bryan.

The wave of anxiety about press standards triggered by this series of revelations – perhaps the greatest of the 'spikes in public concern' Leveson refers to in the introduction to his report – culminated in the two Calcutt reviews commissioned by the Conservative government in the early 1990s. The first of these reports recommended the replacement of the Press Council with a new Press Complaints Commission (PCC), which was given 18 months to prove that self-regulation could work. Both the Committee and the government indicated that this was 'the last chance for the industry to put its own house in order' (quoted in Leveson, 2012a, 211).

By the time Calcutt was commissioned to review the performance of the PCC at the end of this period, the press had succeeded only in intensifying the demands for statutory regulation now stridently ringing out from parliament and the public. Even the broadsheet press was beginning to endorse some form of privacy legislation to curb the excesses of the tabloids and protect the reputation of 'serious' investigative broadsheet journalism. Writing for *The Guardian* following the announcement of the first Calcutt review, Hugo Young argued that it was time 'to end the professional blackmail by which it is pretended that the interests of *The Sun* have anything in common with the interests of *The Guardian*' (quoted in Shannon, 2011, 22).

Here, then, was a near-perfect storm for action. So why, with widespread support for reform converging from across the political spectrum, the public, and even some sections of the press itself, did a British government once again shrink from reform?

At the very point at which the political momentum behind statutory legislation was at its height, a handful of revelations briefly but significantly exposed a rather less clear-cut relationship between public figures and the press than had been assumed by many of those on the side of reform. Despite Princess Diana's claim not to have co-operated with Morton's biography 'in any way' (*Mirror*, 8.6.1992), the Executive Chairman of News International privately disclosed to PCC Chairman Lord McGregor that she had in fact liaised directly with a number of newspaper editors about the serialisation of Morton's biography, heavily annotated Morton's draft, and even arranged for photographs to be taken of herself leaving a friend's house in tears with her children (Shannon, 2011). This information was leaked to the press before the publication of the second Calcutt report and, as *The Times* acknowledged, 'effectively killed the prospect of statutory control of the press' (13.1.1992). McGregor himself admitted that, 'the Princess of Wales had made a mockery of his attempts to protect her against the worst excesses of the tabloid press' (*Times*, 13.1.1992).

Diana was not the only skilful self-publicist operating from inside the royal family; Prince Charles, too, was known to have fed stories to friendly journalists in the ongoing media war between the royal couple (Pimlott, 1998). As a *Times* investigation later found, 'far from being exaggerated, press reports about the death of the royal romance were systematically planted by courtiers operating with scant regard for the health of the fourth estate' (13.1.1993). The Morton controversy revealed a deeply symbiotic relationship between the press and the royal family which political accounts of declining press stan- dards had preferred to gloss over, and, as press historian Adrian Bingham notes, 'drew attention to the way public figures sometimes conspired to invade their own privacy' (2007, 86).

The Paddy Ashdown affair revealed a similar dynamic at work, this time implicating the government itself. Alongside the supposed victimisation of the Princess of Wales, the exposure of the Liberal Democrat leader's affair with his former assistant Tricia Howard had been the other key catalyst in the build-up of support for statutory legislation leading up to the second Calcutt review. The affair had been extensively reported, most memorably by the *Sun* with its famous 'Paddy Pantsdown' headline (6.2.1992). Shortly after the announcement of the second Calcutt review in July 1992, *Sun* editor Kelvin MacKenzie publicly revealed that Ashdown had been the victim of an attempted smear by a senior cabinet minister, who had approached MacKenzie with the names and addresses of three women who had allegedly been involved with the Liberal Democrat leader. In a front-page editorial, *The Sun* proclaimed:

> Well we've got news for Mr. John Major ... Before he accuses the press of unscrupu- lous behaviour he should look closer to home. In the second week of the General Election campaign, a prominent member of the Cabinet phoned *The Sun* with names and addresses of three women. He claimed they had been having affairs with Mr Ashdown. (Quoted in Snoddy, 1992, 215)

Having given the press 'one last chance' to put its house in order, the government's own house was exposed as being none too orderly itself.

In both cases, then, public figures who had been held up, either individually or collectively, as victims of press intrusion, had been revealed to be strategically exploiting this dynamic for political gain. MacKenzie's action briefly exposed a symbiotic relationship that had hitherto been hidden, but also hinted at the damaging consequences of conflict with the tabloids that statutory legislation would undoubtedly provoke. This aspect of the regulation debate was not lost on the Conservatives – indeed, even before MacKenzie's revelation, Lord Deedes acknowledged in the House of Lords that,

> … at the risk of causing hurt looks from my own front bench, I see no likelihood of this government giving much encouragement to legislation which will antagonise the press … The press did the government pretty well in the previous election … No government in their senses bite the hand they feel has fed them. For that and other reasons … this talk of legislation carries with it a great deal of bluff. (Parliamentary Debates (Lords), vol. 538, 1.7.1992, cols. 779–81)

The belief that the Conservatives could not afford to alienate the tabloids, and in so doing risk losing the support that many believed had been instrumental in winning them the 1992 general election, was widely held both within the party and amongst the press. As one 'top Fleet Street executive' put it, 'The Tory Party and Tory Central Office owes a debt. It may be a debt that has to be called in' (quoted in Shannon, 2011, 95).

Statutory legislation: a Damoclean sword

What we have seen of David Cameron's response to Lord Leveson's recommendations places him firmly in this line of previous leaders, all of whom have, in the words of Lord Mandelson, been too 'cowed' by the press to risk taking action that might jeopardise their electoral standing. Even the thinly-veiled implication of horse-trading hinted at by the 'top Fleet Street executive' quoted above is not melodramatic in the present circumstances. Just weeks after the publication of the Leveson Report, *The Telegraph* reported that an aide to Culture Secretary Maria Miller had explicitly 'flagged up' her minister's role in implementing Leveson's recommendations in direct response to a *Telegraph* investigation into her parliamentary expenses (11.12.2012). Such incidents offer tiny insights into how the threat – but never the implementation – of statutory legislation has been used by governments as a direct bargaining tool for keeping revelations of ministerial scandal in check. In many ways, the threat of statutory legislation is the one remaining power that governments still wield over the press – making the prospect of surrendering that power ever more unpalatable.

At one point in his Report, Lord Leveson suggests that 'the response to this Report will itself open a new chapter in the history of the relations between politicians and the press' (Leveson, 2012b, 29). Yet historical precedent – and Cameron's disinclination to part with it – suggests that the next phase of this story will be marked more by continuity than change. Indeed, the Report is full of hints that Leveson himself is only too aware of the fragility of his recommendations. It is significant that the Report summary ends on a clear note of warning, sounded through a carefully selected quotation from John Major's evidence to the inquiry:

> It is important that whatever is recommended is taken seriously by Parliament, and it is infinitely more likely to be enacted if neither of the major parties decides to play partisan short-term party politics with it by seeking to court the favour of an important media baron who may not like what is proposed. (Quoted in Leveson, 2012b, 31)

The Leveson inquiry may yet prove to be the final reckoning in a saga that has spanned three decades and five premierships. However, the realisation of reform will ultimately depend on the ability and willingness of party leaders to break free of the power relationship that has dominated the last 30 years of British politics.

Helena See has worked as a researcher at the think tank Policy Connect and the gay rights charity Stonewall.

References

Bingham, A. (2007) 'Drinking in the last chance saloon', *Media History* 13 (1): 79-92.

Franklin, B. and Petley, J. (1996) 'Killing the age of innocence: newspaper reporting of the death of James Bulger', in Pilcher, J. and Wagg, S. (eds.) *Thatcher's Children? Politics, Childhood and Society in the 1980s and 1990s*, London, Routledge.

Gripsrud, J. (2000) 'Tabloidisation, popular journalism and democracy', in Sparks, C. and Tulloch, J. (eds.) *Tabloid Tales: Global Debates Over Media Standards*, Lanham, MD, Rowman & Littlefield.

Leveson, B. (2012a) *An Inquiry into the Culture, Practices and Ethics of the Press*, London, HM Stationery Office.

Leveson, B. (2012b) *An Inquiry into the Culture, Practices and Ethics of the Press: Executive Summary and Recommendations*, London, HM Stationery Office.

Major, J. (1993) speech at Conservative Party Conference, 8.10.1993, at http://www.johnmajor.co.uk/page1096.html.

Pimlott, B. (1998) 'Monarchy and the message', in Seaton, J. (ed.) *Politics and the Media; Harlots and Prerogatives at the Turn of the Millennium*, Oxford, Blackwell.

Shannon, R. (2011) *A Press Free and Responsible; Self-Regulation and the Press Complaints Commission 1991–2001*, London, John Murray.

Smith, A. M. (1994) *New Right Discourse on Race and Sexuality; Britain, 1968–1990*, Cambridge, Cambridge University Press.

Snoddy, R. (1992) *The Good, the Bad, and the Unacceptable,* London, Faber and Faber.

Thomas, J. (2005) *Popular Newspapers, the Labour Party and British Politics*, London, Routledge.

Leveson, press freedom and the watchdogs

Jacob Rowbottom

In November 2012, Lord Justice Leveson delivered his report on the culture, practices and ethics of the press. In the report, he sets out proposals for reform in a number of areas, including data protection, media lobbying, and relations with the police. However, most attention has focused on the proposal for a new system of self-regulation. Leveson recommends that a new body replace the Press Complaints Commission, which, unlike its predecessor, will have the power to impose financial sanctions in some cases. The new body would not have any statutory powers, but Leveson proposes that a law should set out criteria to assess whether the new regulator is effective and sufficiently independent of the press, parliament and the government. That law should also 'provide a mechanism to recognise and certify' that the new self-regulatory body fulfills the criteria (Leveson, 2012, 1772). The mechanism Leveson proposes is for a 'recognition body' to apply the criteria to the regulator, as part of an assessment taking place at least once every three years. The report therefore does not call for a regulator to be set up by statute (as is the case with broadcasting). Nor does it propose that legislation should actually set out the detailed standards for the press to live up to. Instead, the role for legislation is one step removed. Under the proposals, legislation will set out the criteria to evaluate the regulator and empower the body that certifies the regulator. That is the central part of the 'statutory underpinning' that will be the focus for discussion here (1).

Much of the debate in the immediate aftermath of the report focused on the statutory underpinning. *The Daily Mail* wrote that Leveson 'seems worryingly unable to grasp that once MPs and the media quango become involved, the freedom of the Press from state control will be fatally compromised for the first time since 1694' (*Daily Mail*, 2012). Along similar lines, *The Daily Telegraph* wrote:

> it would be wrong to use bad behaviour by the minority as an excuse to introduce the first press statute since censorship laws were abolished in 1695. Whatever the judge hopes, this would be a slippery slope to state meddling. (*Daily Telegraph*, 2012)

The Independent also wrote that statutory underpinning is 'not only unnecessary, but undesirable' (*Independent*, 2012). Most famously, the Prime Minister told the House of Commons that legislation would cross 'the Rubicon of writing elements of press regulation into the law of the land' (House of Commons debates, 2012a, col. 449). By contrast, the supporters of Leveson are dismissive of such concerns and point out that the reforms require minimal legislative input.

In the fierce debate that has followed Leveson, arguments about press freedom have been strategically advanced to further political goals. It is sometimes difficult to see which claims are the hyperbole of political rhetoric, and which should give genuine cause for concern. A further difficulty in assessing the debate lies in the fact that much argument has focused on the form of press regulation, rather than the substantive question of what the new regulator will actually do. There are, however, important issues of principle and the form of regulation will be relevant to its effectiveness. To assess the arguments underlying the debate on statutory underpinning, it is worth reflecting on the meaning of press freedom.

The nature of press freedom

Early on in the report, Leveson distinguishes freedom of speech, as held by individuals, from freedom of the press. According to Leveson, the former is about self-expression and 'has its roots in a very personal conception of what it is to be human' (Leveson, 2012, 62). The same is not true of mass media institutions, which are 'not human beings with a personal need to be able to self-express' (Leveson, 2012, 62). He is certainly right to draw this distinction, and it is a difference that also reflects our concerns about the power of the media to reach a mass audience on a regular basis. The traditional mass media, that is newspapers and broadcasters, operate in a one-to-many paradigm. Yet those media institutions that reach a mass audience can only accommodate a limited number of speakers (2). Consequently, we justify press freedom not because we think it so overwhelmingly important that a select group of media owners and professionals get the chance to vent, say what they want to a mass audience, or develop their personalities. It is difficult to justify a freedom in terms of its personal benefits to the speaker when, in practice, only a limited group can exercise that freedom.

If the justification for press freedom does not lie in the speaker's right to self-expression, then instead it tends to be justified by its service to the audience or to the public as a whole. There are many varieties of this argument, some of which stress the functions that the mass media perform in a democracy. Most common are arguments that media freedom is necessary to provide information to the public, to hold the powerful to account, to represent a range of diverse viewpoints, and so on. Taking this approach, Leveson stresses the instrumental value of freedom of the press, as something to be 'promoted and protected to the extent that it is with the result that it is thereby enabled to flourish commercially as a sector and to serve its important democratic functions' (Leveson, 2012, 63). Note that he says press freedom is to be protected 'to the extent' that it furthers these goals, suggesting that where this is not the case then limits may be acceptable. Furthermore, insofar as press freedom is based on a concern for the 'community's welfare', it is something that can be balanced with other factors (Dworkin, 1985, 386-7). If this is the case, then it opens the door to arguments that some regulation of the press is necessary to protect other rights and interests.

Even though the instrumental justification comes with these limitations, the critics of Leveson tend to share this approach to press freedom. Newspaper editorials frequently trumpet the important role of the media in its service to democracy. Despite the implicit limits, this argument offers some advantages to the media. First, by emphasising its service to a democracy, the argument helps to legitimise media power. Second, by separating press freedom from individual freedom of speech, the argument can be relied upon by the media to claim special privileges (Dworkin, 1985, 386). For example, newspapers and periodicals are exempt from the election spending controls that apply not only to candidates and parties, but also to any person that wishes to use their economic resources on electoral campaigning. In that example, the instrumental role of the press as serving democracy is advanced to justify its special status in elections.

The democratic functions of the press

Leveson and his opponents therefore seem to share the instrumental understanding of press freedom. However, the different reactions to statutory underpinning might still be explained by a different view of the key democratic functions that the media are expected to perform. The central concern to the opponents of statutory underpinning is the independence of the press from government. There are a number of reasons why the independence of the press might be valued, but the most commonly asserted reason by those opposing statutory underpinning emphasises the 'watchdog' or 'checking' function of the press. For example, the website for the Free Speech Network writes that:

> The press exists to scrutinise those in positions of power. It could not fulfill that role if those it was scrutinising had authority, however apparently limited, over it. (Free Speech Network, 2012)

A similar argument was put forward in an editorial in *The Daily Telegraph*:

> A free press may be unruly, untamed and occasionally unpalatable, but it is the best defence against abuses of power that would otherwise have gone unchecked. (*Daily Telegraph*, 2013)

According to the opponents of the Leveson proposals, we should be particularly wary of any use of statute in the system of press regulation, for fear that politicians might use legislative power to dampen scrutiny of its activities. On this view, statute creates a kind of umbilical link between the press and the state, which might serve as a channel of pressure (as Helena See points out in this issue of *Renewal*, the very threat of statutory regulation can itself be used to place pressure on media outlets).

Invoking the watchdog role of the press provides a powerful argument. The courts have identified this role as being central to press freedom on a number of occasions (for example, *Times Newspapers v UK*, 2009, [40] and [45]). It is also an argument with a long history. In 1704, Matthew Tindal described the press as 'a faithful Sentinel'. In the Cato Letters, press freedom was referred to as 'the great bulwark of liberty', which 'is the terror of traytors and oppressors, and a barrier against them'. Fifty years later, Junius wrote that the press are 'the Palladium of all the civil, political, and religious rights of an Englishman'. In Bentham's work, the press acted as the key organ of a 'Public Opinion Tribunal', which keeps a check on government power. In the nineteenth century, monitoring those in power was a function assigned to the press as the 'fourth estate'. In more recent times, uncovering abuses of power has remained central to the self-image of the press, with Watergate providing a high point. In the last three hundred years, the system of government may have changed dramatically, but appeals to the watchdog function have had an enduring role in arguments for press freedom.

The watchdog argument also fits with most democratic theories. It is not premised on an idealistic or demanding theory of democracy, in which citizens are supposed to use the press to become well informed on most major issues. Those democratic theories that posit a minimal role for the individual citizen – reduced largely to choosing leaders at an election and having limited political knowledge – still have a role for a watchdog press. On this account, the press are needed to sound the alarm if politicians abuse their powers, in order for voters to know when to punish bad behaviour. According to Michael Schudson, the watchdog function does not even require that all voters pay attention to these alarms, but simply that politicians 'believe that some people somewhere are following the news' (Schudson, 2008, 14). On this view, it is politicians' belief that they are being monitored that deters abuses of power. However, the watchdog function is not limited to the minimal theories of democracy. The more demanding approaches to democracy will still hope that the press reveal abuses of power, while performing other functions (Baker, 2002). The watchdog role has a wide appeal.

An analogy with the separation of powers is sometimes made to explain why the independence of the press is so important to the watchdog function. Justice Stewart, of the US Supreme Court, wrote that the US Constitution guarantees press freedom 'to create a fourth institution outside the Government as an additional check on the three official branches' (Stewart, 1975, 634). The idea of the press acting as a quasi-constitutional check is not limited to the US. In a recent pamphlet, Tim Luckhurst argued that the checking function is all the more important in the UK given the lack of a formal separation of powers between executive and legislature (Luckhurst, 2012, 27). The point is not new. While Bentham criticised the doctrine of the separation of powers in the formal institutions of the state, he argued that public opinion was 'the only check' on 'the pernicious exercise of the power of government' (Bentham, 1983).

Of course, there are other reasons why the independence of the press might be valued. If government (or any other powerful actor) can influence the press, there is a concern that the flow of information will be distorted. The powerful actor might seek to ensure a particular story is given higher prominence than it deserves or withhold important stories from public view. Such distortion can be seen to undermine the free competition of ideas and arguments in public debate. However, Justice Stewart distinguishes his watchdog argument from a 'marketplace of ideas' justification for press freedom, as the latter might allow for greater government regulation of the press to improve the flow of ideas, such as a statutory right of reply law (Stewart, 1975). On Stewart's view, a right of reply law would violate press freedom. C. Edwin Baker, explaining such a contrast, notes that the watchdog argument does not aim to promote diverse information, but rather seeks to protect 'a source that the government does not control' (Baker, 1989, 233).

It is unsurprising that Leveson himself cited the watchdog role as one of the democratic functions of the press (Leveson, 2012, 65). In one part of his report, Leveson also uses an analogy with the separation of powers. He recommends that the law should 'place an explicit duty on the Government to uphold and protect the freedom of the press' (Leveson, 2012, 1781). In making such a recommendation, Leveson follows a similar clause in the Constitutional Reform Act 2005, which requires ministers to uphold judicial independence. We may, however, question the effectiveness of such a clause. The duty to respect judicial independence has certainly not stopped some ministers from criticising court decisions in the strongest terms, and it is not clear that a press freedom clause will be any more effective. Putting this doubt aside, the proposed clause shows how the independence of the press is seen as part of the separation of powers, requiring arrangements that are analogous to those protecting other branches of government.

So far, the watchdog function for the press appears to be an area of agreement between Leveson and his critics. Both see it as a key role for the press. The difference in their positions might be explained if we distinguish between a 'moderate' and a 'strong' form of the watchdog argument. The moderate version of the argument sees the watchdog function as one among several functions of the press, and requires that we assess whether any laws applying to the press will potentially inhibit that function. This form of the argument can be used to call for a public interest defence to defamation actions or to criminal law controls. It does not, however, stand against any laws involving the press.

Under this position, the question is not whether statute should be used to implement Leveson, but what the terms of that statute will be. By contrast, a strong form of the argument views the watchdog function as the preeminent role of the press and demands a clear structural separation between press and government. It emphasises the need for a clear separation of powers and assumes parliamentary or government input will threaten press independence. This strong view may explain why some see statute as a Rubicon that should not be crossed. It provides a prophylactic rule, which seeks to act as a barrier between press and government.

The central difficulty with the strong version of the argument is that it prioritises the threat to press freedom posed by state institutions. However, press independence can be jeopardised by private power too. Aside from government, the media can be subject to pressures from markets and from advertisers. Editorial judgment can be influenced by proprietorial pressure. In these cases, some input from the state might help bolster press freedom from these influences. For example, a law requiring certain media entities to guarantee editorial independence or include a conscience clause in journalists' contracts might promote the independence of the press from private pressures. While a strong form of the watchdog argument might object to such interventions in the internal affairs of the press, the moderate version would be more willing to accommodate such proposals. A similar debate sometimes arises in relation to state subsidies for the press, with a moderate view accepting that such subsidies can aid independence (if structured in the right way), but with a strong view suspicious of the idea.

Those making a strong watchdog argument might reply that we should show greater concern about government interferences with press freedom, and that tolerating some scope for private interference is a price which must be paid in order to minimise the threat of government control. Such an answer is premised on a mistrust of government. This mistrust manifests itself in two ways. First is a view that the watchdog function of the press is primarily about monitoring state actors. It assumes that state power is the main threat to people's liberty and is where the checking function is needed most. Secondly, because the press is guarding against abuses of state power, the most important aspect of its independence is the structural protection from the state. The argument then runs that if we mistrust officials and assume that, where there is an opportunity, power will be abused, then we should not trust those officials with a power that could be used to stifle public criticism and prevent exposure of their wrongdoings. On this view, state interventions in the press, even when made for good reasons, pose a risk of harm greater than that posed by private sources of power. By taking these steps, the strong form of the instrumental watchdog argument can be constructed into a libertarian appeal to press freedom (3).

The Leveson proposals

Against this background, it is interesting to look at some of the arguments that have been advanced against statutory underpinning. One argument is that any form of state input will allow politicians to influence the regulator, and thereby impose some control on the press. For example, in the House of Commons debate, Peter Lilley expressed the concern that the recognition body may use its power of certification to pressure the regulator to 'follow either the Government's prejudices or its own' (House of Commons debates, 2012b, col. 662). This line of argument suggests that the power to certify will jeopardise the independence of the regulator.

Those taking the strong version of the watchdog argument would accept this argument on the assumption that any type of state input poses such a risk. By contrast, the moderate version treats this issue as one concerning the design of the statute, rather than as an argument against any statute. Take, for example, the proposed legislative criteria to be applied by the recognition body when deciding whether the self-regulatory body is sufficiently independent and effective. Leveson proposes the criteria should include the self-regulatory body having a code of practice for the press that takes into account free speech, while also providing standards to deal with the conduct of the press, to show appropriate respect for privacy and to provide for accuracy (Leveson, 2012, 1763). This might be thought to raise two issues. First, the legislative criteria may give scope for politicians to indicate which standards the press must fulfill. The criteria proposed by Leveson is, however, stated at a level of generality and includes matters that would most likely have been included in the new code in any event (and which are already included in the Press Complaints Commission Code). If this were still cause for concern, the criteria relating to the code could be less specific. For example, Labour's draft bill on implementing Leveson, published in December, omits any reference to protecting privacy in its criteria relating to the code of practice. The criteria in Lord Lester's bill to implement Leveson are at an even greater level of generality, for example in asking that the new regulator encourage and maintain 'high professional standards and good practices' and deal with 'professional misconduct'. The merits of the different formulations can be debated, but the point is that the statute can frame the criteria in a way that is not overly prescriptive.

The second concern is that even if the legislation provides only very general criteria, the recognition body might use its power to influence the direction of the regulator. For example, the recognition body could refuse to certify the regulator if it believes the code fails to protect free speech or fails to set high enough standards. Yet the terms of the Leveson proposals do not create a 'procedure that provides for structured, authoritative government pronouncements regarding the performance of the press', which is the core concern of one leading proponent of the watchdog theory (Blasi, 1977, 590). Recognition and certification is a very blunt tool that operates by looking at the workings of the system of regulation as a whole. It would not be used to express a verdict on a particular newspaper or even a particular decision from the regulator. Furthermore, the decision by the recognition body would be limited to the criteria in the statute and its conclusions would be reasoned. Finally, the process would not offer a government pronouncement, as long as the recognition body is independent of government. This independence would depend on how the recognition body is appointed. Leveson at first proposed that Ofcom should perform this function, but, due to concerns about that body having a government-appointed director, that possibility now seems to be off the table. Instead, negotiations are focused on an alternative body to perform this role, with some proposing members of the judiciary. The point being made is that the statute can be drafted in such a way as to minimise the scope for government or parliamentary influence. The argument against any statutory input seems to be premised on a level of mistrust, which suggests even the most limited risk is not worth taking.

Another argument against statutory underpinning is that even if the legislation starts off as modest, there is nothing to stop it being amended and extended into more onerous forms of legislation (see Maria Miller, House of Commons Debates, 2012b, col. 598). This is a type of slippery slope argument. Again, it is a view premised on a concern that any precedent for legislating in this area, no matter how well-intentioned, is likely to be abused by some future government. If this is a concern, then it is one that can apply to a range of others laws, which could all be amended to make life for the press more difficult, such as the Contempt of Court Act 1981 or the Defamation Bill (still going through Parliament at the time of writing). The risk of politicians interfering with press content is more direct with the examples of contempt of court and defamation, as Parliament actually decides in those laws what detailed standards the press has to fulfill. In the Leveson proposals, Parliament will not set those standards. Furthermore, the Communications Act 2003 creates a system of content regulation for broadcasters. If statute constitutes the Rubicon, it appears to have been crossed already. Maybe the Leveson proposals can be distinguished from these examples, as Leveson proposes a new system of regulation specific to the press. However, if the concern is only with certain types of statute, then those types of statute need to be identified before we can formulate a prophylactic rule. In any event, Parliament is subject to some checks and any statutory amendments made in future could be subject to challenge under the Human Rights Act 1998 if it unduly interferes with press freedom.

We might reject the outright opposition to any statute to implement Leveson partly because we do not prioritise the risks of state power to the exclusion of concerns about other sources of power. The press needs to check private sources of power and therefore needs independence from powerful private actors. If we take the view that private sources of power can be detrimental to press freedom, it becomes clear why the system of regulation needs to have some independence from the industry. Just as there are dangers with government pressuring a regulator to decide an issue one way or another, there are also dangers that the industry could pressure the regulator to make decisions that are favourable to its commercial interests. The Leveson proposal therefore seeks to mediate between these competing pressures. The press has some say in so far as it can choose whether to join the regulatory scheme. The body will be self-regulatory and established by the press. However, the statutory recognition process seeks to ensure that these connections with the industry do not undermine the regulatory body and that it remains sufficiently independent. The system combines statutory underpinning and input from the industry, in the hope that neither source of power exerts control over the regulator. There might be risks with government or parliamentary input, but there are ways of reducing those risks. If a system is to be established that allows for some state support, and does not leave the industry to regulate itself, then this is a risk that needs to be taken.

So far, the choice seems to be between some form of statutory underpinning or allowing the press to continue to regulate itself. The Conservative Party has successfully sought to advance a separate approach that avoids this stark choice, by underpinning the new regulator through a Royal Charter. Given the Conservatives' stance against statute, this proposal is somewhat surprising. It is puzzling that, having advanced arguments that any statute would undermine press freedom, all these objections to state input seem to be abandoned in relation to a prerogative power. The libertarian approach described is concerned with state input in whatever form. According to that view, even with a Royal Charter, the psychological barrier to state action would be crossed and the apparatus to support the regulatory system, once established, could be tinkered with in future. Given this, it is difficult to see why a Charter is more acceptable for the strong view of the watchdog argument than statute.

The Conservative Party, subsequently followed by Labour and the Liberal Democrats, have argued that there are ways a Charter could be protected from subsequent amendment by the executive, through provision that amendments can only be made with approval of the leaders of the three main parties and by a resolution in Parliament. Even if a Charter could be protected from future amendment by prerogative powers, Parliament would still have the power to legislate to override provisions of the Charter or impose new obligations on the recognition body. The attempts to entrench the Charter would therefore not so much fortify the Rubicon, but create a Maginot Line that would be easily by-passed through legislative means. If cross-party agreement is desirable before any changes are made to the new system, this could be achieved in relation to legislation through a constitutional convention. So the Charter does not seem to offer an advantage over legislation. It can also offer some disadvantages in so far as it gives greater scope for the terms of the system for recognition and certification to be decided behind closed doors through bargaining between interested parties (and that bargaining would produce an outcome which the Conservative proposals would then seek partly to entrench). While it is undesirable for MPs to influence the regulator, there is something to be said for using the legislative process that would allow MPs to scrutinise properly and publicly debate the general framework of the recognition system.

Relations between politicians and the press

The threat to press independence does not only come from formal legal interventions. If senior media figures and politicians develop close ties in which each can offer the other mutual benefits, then the watchdog role is compromised. While distinct from statutory power, this informal link could lead to a situation where the press holds back on a story or does the bidding of the government on a particular issue. While Leveson found no evidence of any backroom deals between politicians and senior media representatives, he concludes that the relationship had become 'too close' (Leveson, 2012, 1439). As with judicial independence, Leveson states that in the absence of any direct collusion, there is at least a problem with 'public perceptions' that independence is being jeopardised (Leveson, 2012, 1439). Consequently, Leveson calls on the party leaders to devise stronger transparency rules in relation to communications with senior media executives and their agents. He argues that this should go beyond recording details of formal meetings and should include some information about informal communications, such as email.

It would be difficult to go any further than this. Lobbying can provide important information to ministers and civil servants, and there will be a need for senior media executives to communicate with government at times. This shows that a complete separation between press and politicians is not possible, and the two often rely on each other to perform their functions. Transparency at least provides a way to monitor the extent of the communications. However, it also shows that greater self-restraint should perhaps be shown by politicians and the press. In his discussion of lobbying by the press, Leveson's criticism focuses on the politicians, finding that they had acted in ways that have 'not served the public interest' (Leveson, 2012, 1439). Leveson states that the issue raised by lobbying is the accountability of politicians, not 'the conduct of the press' (Leveson, 2012, 1451). By taking this view, Leveson places all responsibility on the politicians and treats the press like any other private enterprise that seeks to advocate its interests forcefully. This view, however, overlooks the claim made by the media that they are different from other industries and that they perform a quasi-constitutional function in holding government to account. If the press are to have such a role, then they too have a responsibility to show caution in developing close links with government on matters of policy. Certainly, if the press is seen to be too close to government, then they risk undermining the legitimacy of their claim to act as a quasi-constitutional check. The closeness of press and government therefore poses a real challenge to the watchdog function.

Conclusion

It is easy to write off much of the debate following the Leveson Report as self-interested positioning by the media industry or privacy campaigners. Claims being made about press freedom are being advanced in the context of political advocacy and should not be taken at face value. However, this essay has sought to identify the understanding of press freedom that underlies the criticism of the Leveson proposals for statutory underpinning. The criticisms appear to fit most closely with a structural understanding of press freedom as guaranteeing an absence of state interference. There are lessons that can be taken from this argument, in particular in understanding the risks that statute may pose. This does not mean stopping at any imagined Rubicon concerning the use of legislation. Instead, it entails that we seek to frame legislation in a way that minimises those risks – though this should not be used as an excuse to water down the Leveson proposals simply to please the industry.

This essay has looked at one argument concerning the use of statute. There are many other parts of the Leveson proposals that need consideration, such as the impact of the incentives for joining the new regulator. Once the new regulator is established, the impact of its code of practice will also need to be evaluated in the light of its effect on the watchdog function. While important, the watchdog role is not the only democratic function of the press. Those other functions might on occasion call for a different relationship with the legislature and executive. Ultimately, the argument here is that concern about mistrust of government power, while important, should not be taken to an extreme that precludes any measures seeking to address abuses of other sources of power. While the protection for speech under the US First Amendment is often associated with a mistrust of government, the culture in the UK is different and shows 'more concern about the excessive power of media magnates to influence public opinion' (Feldman, 1998, 170). That means we should address abuses of private sources of power, including the press. If there is one lesson to take from Leveson it is that as well as emphasising the checking function of the press, we also ask what checks the press are subject to.

Jacob Rowbottom is Fellow in Law at University College, Oxford. He is the author of *Democracy Distorted* (Cambridge University Press, 2010).

References

Baker, C. E. (1989) *Human Liberty and Freedom of Speech*, Oxford, Oxford University Press.

Baker, C. E. (2002) *Media, Markets and Democracy*, Cambridge, Cambridge University Press.

Bentham, J. (1983) *Constitutional Code*, edited by Rosen, F. and Burns J. H., Oxford, Clarendon.

Blasi, V. (1977) 'The checking value in First Amendment theory', 2 *American Bar Foundation Research Journal* 521.

Daily Mail (2012) 'Daily Mail comments', *Daily Mail* 30.11.2012.

Daily Telegraph (2012) 'Let us implement Leveson, without a press law', *Daily Telegraph* 30.11.2012.

Daily Telegraph (2013) 'Putting self-interest ahead of press freedom', *Daily Telegraph* 20.2.2013.

Dworkin, R. (1985) *A Matter of Principle*, Oxford, Clarendon Press.

Feldman, D. (1998) 'Content neutrality', in Loveland, I. (ed.) *Importing the First Amendment*, Oxford, Hart.

Free Speech Network (2012) Website homepage, at http://freespeechnetwork.wordpress.com/.

House of Commons Debates (2012a) vol. 554, 29.11.2012.

House of Commons Debates (2012b) vol. 554, 3.12.2012.

Independent (2012) 'There is only one flaw in this epic verdict – but it's a crucial flaw', *Independent* 30.11.2012.

Leveson, B. (2012) *An Inquiry into the Culture, Practices and Ethics of the Press*, London, HM Stationary Office.

Luckhurst, T. (2012) *Responsibility Without Power*, Bury St Edmunds, Abramis.

Schudson, M. (2008) *Why Democracies Need an Unlovable Press*, Cambridge, Polity.

Siebert, F., Peterson, T. and Schramm, W. (1956) *Four Theories of the Press*, Urbana, University of Illinois Press.

Stewart, P. (1975) 'Or of the Press', 26 *Hastings Law Journal* 631.

Times Newspapers v UK [2009] ECHR 3002/03.

Notes

1. There are other parts of Leveson's scheme that raise issues of controversy, such as some of the incentives to encourage membership of the new regulator, that are beyond the scope of this article.
2. Of course, the use of comments sections on newspaper websites does open the forum to many other speakers. However, only a relatively small number can contribute to the main articles and set the agenda of the newspaper.
3. Siebert et al. note that the emphasis on the watchdog argument is a distinguishing characteristic of the libertarian view (Siebert et al., 1956, 56).

Essays

The political economy of the service transition

Anne Wren

Over the past thirty years the wealthiest OECD economies – in Europe, North America and Australasia – have experienced rapid de-industrialisation. A range of factors have contributed to the de-industrialisation process: some, like technological change and changes in the characteristics of consumer demand, are internal to the development process in the economies themselves; others, like increased competition from developing countries in the market for manufactured goods, are external. Whatever its roots, there is no doubt that the impact of de-industrialisation on labour markets has been profound: more than three quarters of employment in most OECD countries is now in services, while industrial sectors, on average, account for less than one fifth. This sectoral shift in the locus of economic activity has potentially radical implications for politics and society. In a new book on *The Political Economy of the Service Transition* (Wren, 2013; hereafter: *PET*), I have brought together a group of scholars from Europe and North America to assess the implications of the service transition for existing socio-economic regimes. We investigate how variations in the underlying institutional structures of alternative 'varieties of capitalism' have influenced their ability to manage the transition to services – in particular their capacity for creating new types of jobs in the face of declining opportunities in core manufacturing sectors, and the distributional outcomes with which new strategies for employment creation are associated. We also analyse the implications of the transition for politics – and for the sustainability of existing socio-economic models. The central findings of this volume speak to the on-going debate on the pages of *Renewal* and elsewhere about the viability of alternative 'varieties of capitalism' in a post-crisis world.

In the book we identify a set of critical challenges which de-industrialisation and the transition to services create in the economic and electoral arenas. In this essay, I will outline these challenges in brief, describing what I see as their primary implications for alternative models of capitalism.

The transition to services: economic challenges

One of the most serious socio-economic challenges posed by the de-industrialisation process is a reduction in job opportunities at medium and lower skill levels. The question for governments is: as the core of employment in manufacturing sectors shrinks, how, and where, are new jobs to be created? (Wren, chapter 1, *PET*). At stake in the resolution of this problem, also, is the future of the welfare state: reductions in the number of industrial workers in stable jobs who are contributors to the system threaten the affordability of welfare state provision, unless new jobs can be created in services (Nelson and Stephens, chapter 4, *PET*).

Low-skilled employment and the employment-equality trade-off

One 'solution' to the problem of declining employment opportunities at medium to low skill levels, which has been pursued most aggressively in Liberal regimes like the US and UK over the past few decades, has been to facilitate the expansion of low-skilled (and low-paid) private sector employment in personal, consumer, and social services. These countries have enjoyed considerable success in terms of employment creation in these sectors in recent decades. However, there are marked downsides to the strategy which they have pursued.

The first is that it has been heavily reliant on keeping relative wages in low-skilled service sectors low. The demand for personal and consumer services is very responsive to changes in prices (this is unsurprising when we consider their capacity for home production – think of catering and gardening services, for example). However, the capacity for productivity increases in the provision of these kinds of services is low (waitressing and childcare are good examples to think through here – it might be possible to increase the number of children supervised by one carer, the number of tables served by one waiter and so on, but in the process the quality of care and service will almost certainly decline). Given a low capacity for productivity growth, it becomes particularly important to keep relative wages in these sectors low, in order to generate a demand expansion based on the high price elasticity of demand for these kinds of services. As a result it is harder to combine the expansion of lower-skilled service employment with equality than it was during the so-called 'golden age' of manufacturing expansion in the 1950s and 1960s (Iversen and Wren, 1998). (When the simultaneous occurrence of high demand elasticities for new consumer durables, and high rates of productivity growth in manufacturing sectors engendered by Fordist innovations in production processes, meant that relative prices could be kept low at the same time as real wage rates in these sectors were growing: Meidner, 1974; Rehn, 1985).

In Liberal regimes, then, the dominant response to the trade-off between wage equality and employment creation in low-skilled, low productivity service sectors has been to emphasise the goal of employment creation, with increases in wage inequality facilitated by the removal or reduction of protections on the wages of low-paid workers, attacks on the power of trades unions, and de-centralised wage bargaining.

As the experience of recent years has made clear, however, increasing inequality has not been the only downside of the Liberal strategy for employment growth over the past quarter century. In addition to these supply-side adjustments, there was a strong demand side component to the expansion of employment in low-skilled service sectors in these regimes during this period. Part of this demand resulted from increases in family working hours (as more women entered paid work, and more workers began to work longer hours). Increases in working hours raise the demand for consumer and personal services via a substitution effect (women working in the paid labour force purchasing childcare and catered food, for example), but also via an income effect (families that work more hours earn more money, and personal and consumer services are 'luxury' items which occupy proportionately more of individual and household budgets as incomes rise) (Gregory, Salvadera, and Shettkat, 2007). Both of these effects can be seen as outcomes of structural labour market change, therefore, which are not inherently unsustainable. By the turn of the century, however, the expansion of demand, and of employment, in these sectors was also closely linked to the expansion of cheap consumer credit and the asset (and in particular house) price inflation which accompanied it. Just how important this highly unsustainable element of the employment growth model had become in Liberal regimes by the early part of this century has yet to be accurately assessed: what is clear, however, is that the shock to employment in these countries in the wake of the crisis (when the supply of credit dried up) was relatively severe.

In contrast to the Liberal regimes, in the co-ordinated regimes of central and Northern Europe, levels of coordination in wage setting (and, as a result, levels of wage equality) remain relatively high, and the extent of reliance on employment creation in low paid, low productivity private service sectors in recent decades has been considerably lower. The social democratic regimes of Scandinavia, for example, have (to varying degrees) managed to continue to pursue simultaneously high rates of employment and wage equality by employing large numbers of workers at all skill levels in public service sectors. Meanwhile some continental European regimes – like Germany – have kept unemployment levels down in part by their continued strong performance in traditional export-oriented manufacturing sectors, but also because large proportions of the working age population (and large numbers of women in particular) remain outside the paid labour force. The lower levels of reliance on debt-financed consumer demand in these regimes before the crisis meant that the shock which they experienced when the crisis hit (and credit dried up) was less severe. Meanwhile, the implications for equality of the pursuit of either of these strategies are also more positive than in the case of Liberal regimes – although the inegalitarian nature of strategies which rely on discouraging labour force participation amongst certain segments of the population should not be overlooked.

Critically though, none of these strategies is, on its own, a sufficient long-term solution to the problem of de-industrialisation. Without a thriving set of high value added sectors to finance them, the expansive public service sectors of Scandinavia are ultimately unaffordable. Without the existence of a core group of well-paid workers in high productivity export sectors, the large numbers of early retirees and women working within the home in Germany and other continental European countries cannot be supported. The strategy of expanding employment in low productivity private services, meanwhile, relies not just on low relative prices, but also on rising incomes and, as the Liberal experience of the past decade has shown, an over-reliance on the expansion of credit and 'wealth illusion', rather than productivity and income growth as a basis for the expansion of demand and employment in these sectors, is both unsustainable and economically costly.

Any *sustainable* strategy for employment growth must depend instead on the expansion of output and employment in high productivity sectors and, in the context of de-industrialisation, this means that expansion in high productivity service sectors is increasingly key. So what does this mean in terms of policy?

Skills and high-end service expansion

The revolution in information and communications technologies (ICT) which has taken place over the past three decades has radically transformed production and trade in certain areas of services. In so-called 'knowledge-intensive' sectors – business, finance, and communications, for example – the capacity for productivity growth and for trade have been hugely enhanced by rapid access to large amounts of information, and the ability to communicate that information – both locally and globally – rapidly and cheaply. The transformation has not occurred in all areas of service production. In some sectors (for example the personal and social services discussed earlier) the impact of the new technology is less marked. Primarily this is because the provision of these services is, to varying degrees, reliant on face-to-face human interaction: a computer, for example, cannot increase the number of children that can be effectively supervised by a child care worker, nor can it facilitate her in providing this service to children who are not in her immediate vicinity (i.e. in participating in international trade). In these areas, then, the uptake of the new technology has been relatively low, and these remain essentially low productivity, non-traded sectors. In contrast, in the more knowledge-intensive sectors, where provision is less heavily reliant on face-to-face human interaction, and information and its transmission are at a premium, rates of productivity growth and international trade have increased rapidly.

Given their high capacity for productivity growth and for trade, these 'dynamic' service sectors have a critical role to play in any sustainable strategy for employment creation in the context of de-industrialisation. The important question, then, is what kinds of policies promote expansion in these types of sectors? In our book we place a heavy emphasis on skill formation, and on the capacity of different 'varieties of capitalism' to provide the skills which high-end service markets require. And here, the fact that these sectors are highly ICT-intensive has important implications.

It is by now well-established empirically that ICT and college educated labour are complements in production. As Autor, Levy, and Murnane (2003) point out, the new technology is highly effective at performing routine tasks which can be specified by stored instructions – even where the required programs are highly complex (for example, book-keeping or clerical work). As a result it acts as a substitute for labour in performing these tasks, which are typically carried out by workers at medium-skill levels (those with secondary, or some (but not complete) college education). It is less effective, however, at performing non-routine cognitive tasks requiring 'flexibility, creativity, generalised problem solving, and complex communications' (Autor, Levy, and Murnane, 2003, 5). Rather it serves to complement the skills of the (typically college educated) workers who perform those tasks: faster access to more complete market information, for example, may improve managerial decision-making, but it cannot substitute for that decision-making. Since technology is a complement to, rather than a substitute for, this type of human capital, then, investment in the new technology increases the demand for college educated labour.

Successful expansion in ICT-intensive service sectors is therefore reliant on the existence of an adequate supply of workers with tertiary-level skills. In this regard also the characteristics of the current era of service expansion differ significantly from those of the era of industrial expansion which preceded it. In the 1950s and 1960s, Fordist industrial expansion was associated with an increased demand for labour at low to medium skill levels – and was particularly notable for the existence of complementarities in production between low and high-skilled industrial labour (see, for example, Wallerstein, 1990). In contrast, successful expansion in high-end service sectors requires up-skilling, and increasing the numbers of workers receiving high quality tertiary education. This underscores, of course, the importance of ensuring effective investment at the tertiary level, and also in facilitating tertiary enrolment and access. Recent research indicates, however, that it also implies a critical role for investment in school based learning beginning as early as the pre-primary level, since education at this level is increasingly regarded as a key determinant of tertiary outcomes – especially for children from lower-skilled households (see, for example, Cuhne and Heckman, 2007; Heckman and Jacobs, 2010).

So how well equipped are existing 'varieties of capitalism' to meet the skills demands of the service economy? Liberal regimes have been relatively successful thus far at producing large numbers of high quality college graduates. Levels of public educational investment are low in these countries in relative terms, however, and the system relies on the existence of high levels of wage inequality, which create strong incentives for private educational investment (since the relative rewards for such investment are high), and the extensive use of student loans. One clear downside of the model for those concerned with equity of outcomes, therefore, is that it comes with high levels of wage inequality attached; another is that it has been associated with what look like increasingly unsustainable levels of student debt in recent years (Mitchell, 2012; Stiglitz, 2012). There is also some evidence to suggest that, in spite of the incentives for private investment existing in these regimes, overall levels of educational investment have been insufficient. Goldin and Katz (2008), for example, cite the failure of the US education system to provide an adequate supply of college-educated workers to keep pace with technological change as one of the primary causes of the increase in inequality in that country at the end of the last century, while evidence in our volume indicates that even in the highly decentralised wage-setting environments found in Liberal regimes, increases in public investment in school and college based education have significant positive effects on employment in dynamic service sectors (Wren, Fodor and Theodoropoulou, chapter 3, *PET*).

The countries of central and Northern Europe face a different set of challenges as regards educational policy. Here high levels of co-ordination in wage bargaining ensure much higher levels of wage equality. One effect of this, though, is to reduce the incentives for private individuals to invest in higher level skills – since the relative rewards to such investment are substantially smaller. In these regimes, then, there is a risk of a shortage in the skills on which expansion in high-end knowledge intensive services relies, unless the government steps in to subsidise them (see Ansell and Gingrich, chapter 6; Iversen and Soskice, chapter 2; and Wren, Fodor, and Theodoropoulou, chapter 3, all in *PET*).

In the social democratic regimes of Scandinavia, this is precisely what governments have done – providing high levels of investment in school and college based education all the way from the pre-primary to the tertiary level, which have resulted in high levels of tertiary enrolment and have facilitated the expansion of high-skilled employment in high-end service sectors. This strategy has several potential advantages in terms of equity. It does not rely on the existence of wage-premia for highly skilled workers to induce investment in higher level skills. It can facilitate greater equity of access to tertiary education – in the first place because that education is publicly financed, but also because the public financing of education for school-aged, and even more critically, pre-primary children has knock-on effects on levels of equity in tertiary outcomes for children from different social backgrounds (Heckman and Jacobs, 2010). Finally, investment in early childhood education and care removes some of the costs of caring from women, increasing levels of equity between men and women in terms of access to labour markets, and facilitating women's labour force participation and employment. The question, of course, is whether the implied spending is affordable in an era of 'austerity'. In a context in which higher level skills are increasingly critical to expansion in the dynamic, high-value added sectors of the economy, though, one might equally ask whether countries can afford *not* to undertake investments of this nature. And to the extent that educational investment forms the basis for growth and expansion in high value-added sectors, and the creation of employment in these sectors, this strategy has the potential to be economically self-sustaining.

In contrast to the Scandinavian social democratic regimes, some continental European countries – like Germany – have combined high levels of co-ordination in wage setting (and equality) with lower levels of public investment in tertiary and schools based education, and levels of tertiary enrolment are relatively low. In the past of course, as Hall and Soskice (2001) have influentially argued, this formed part of a highly effective educational strategy in which large proportions of the workforce participated in apprenticeship based vocational training regimes which equipped workers with strong firm and sector-specific skills and formed the basis for comparative advantage in core areas of industrial production (for example, capital goods). The question, however, is whether this strategy remains sustainable in an era in which employment expansion increasingly relies on exploiting the complementarities between ICT and college educated labour. Even in Germany, the archetype of the successful apprenticeship-based political economy, the proportion of workers employed in high-skilled industrial jobs has declined sharply in recent decades.

Challenges in the political arena

The structural change engendered by the transition to services is not confined to the economic arena. Our research indicates that the transition is also associated with shifts in political demographics which have important implications for electoral outcomes in general, and for welfare state politics in particular. These changes also stem directly from the transformation of labour markets.

First, we find that the transition to services has changed the extent to which workers at different skill levels are exposed to international markets. Half a century ago, workers at lower skill levels were more likely to be employed in sectors which were exposed to international market forces than their higher skilled counterparts. This was because employment at lower skill levels was heavily concentrated in (typically internationally traded) manufacturing sectors, while employment at higher skill levels was more concentrated in (typically untraded) service professions (such as medicine, government, and the law). Our data shows, however, that one effect of the ICT revolution, and the expansion of high skilled employment in internationally traded service sectors like business and finance over the past two decades, has been to significantly increase the proportion of highly skilled workers who are employed in internationally exposed sectors (as the numbers of highly trained workers finding employment in these sectors increases). In contrast, at the lower end of the skill spectrum, the dominant effect of de-industrialisation has been a decline in the proportion of workers employed in internationally traded manufacturing sectors and an increasing concentration of employment in sheltered service sectors (non-traded personal or consumer services and the public sector).

These changes may not seem particularly noteworthy, but in fact they have important political implications. Our analysis of public opinion data indicates that highly skilled workers employed in sectors which are exposed to the global economy are significantly less supportive of welfare state spending and redistribution than their counterparts at similar skill levels working in sheltered sectors: they are also less likely to vote for left parties (Rehm and Wren, chapter 8, *PET*). We attribute this variation in part to a perception amongst workers in exposed sectors that levels of welfare state spending which are too high pose a threat to competitiveness and, ultimately, to their employment. Of course this (real or imagined) threat must be balanced against the benefits of welfare state spending in terms of public service provision and income guarantees. However, for workers at higher incomes, the net benefits of social policy are less likely to outweigh the cost, especially where the perceived threat to their employment and income through lost competitiveness is high, with the result that they are less favourable to welfare state spending and redistribution, and less likely to vote for parties of the left.

Highly-skilled and highly-paid workers in sheltered sectors, in contrast, are less likely to perceive that welfare state spending poses a threat to their jobs – and indeed if they are employed in the public sector itself they clearly rely on such spending for their own employment. As a result, these kinds of workers are more likely to support higher levels of welfare state provision, and more likely to vote for left parties. At lower skill levels, we find little significant difference in the preferences of workers in exposed and sheltered workers. It is well established that income is one of the primary determinants of levels of support for social policy (and unsurprising given that the net benefits of social policy typically decline as incomes increase). At lower incomes, therefore, it appears that the net benefits of social policy in terms of income and welfare guarantees outweigh the risks of employment loss even for workers in exposed sectors, so that their preferences roughly align with their sheltered counterparts.

This is important because it reduces the capacity for cross-class consensus in support of the welfare state, and left parties. Whereas previously highly-skilled workers employed in sheltered service sectors provided a critical anchor in cross-class coalitions in support of left-leaning economic platforms, the movement of significant numbers of highly skilled workers out of these sectors and into internationally exposed private sectors threatens to undermine these coalitions (since levels of support for welfare state spending and left parties are typically lower amongst these groups). Moreover, additional findings in the volume suggest that other changes in labour markets closely associated with the increased economic dominance of this kind of sector may have similar kinds of implications – for example, we find that workers who work more hours than the typical working week (common in many high end service sectors) are also less favourable to various redistributive policies and to left parties than their colleagues (at similar skill and income levels) who work shorter hours (Barnes, chapter 9, *PET*).

Bad news for the left and for the welfare state then? The good news, however, relates to the other dominant aspect of the transformation of labour markets in service based economies – that is, of course, the rapid increase in the number of female labour force participants. Female labour force participation closely tracks the expansion of service sector employment, and the indications are that causality in this relationship runs in both directions. On the one hand, women have a comparative advantage in service sector jobs in which they are not disadvantaged, either by a premium on 'brawn', or by labour market experiences which may be interrupted (since service sectors are less heavily reliant on firm and sector specific skills acquired through long-term experience within a particular firm or sector, and are reliant instead on more general skills, typically acquired initially through schools and college based learning, and more easily transferable across firms and sectors) (Iversen and Rosenbluth, 2010 and chapter 10, *PET*). On the other hand, increases in female labour market participation in themselves clearly increase the demand for services which might otherwise be provided in the home (such as, for example, childcare, cleaning, and catering).

Whatever its roots, the relationship between service sector expansion and female employment is a tight one. The importance of this for politics is that women who participate in the labour market are significantly more supportive of welfare state policies involving public employment and service provision. Public service expansion serves simultaneously to provide female employment and to facilitate female labour market participation (by supporting women in the caring roles for which they typically share a disproportionate amount of the burden like child and elder care). As a result, women who participate in the labour market now show higher levels of support for these policies, and for the left parties that advocate them, than men; they are also more left-leaning than women who do not participate. And as a result, the size of the gender gap in political preferences is increasing over time in line with rising rates of female labour force participation (Iversen and Rosenbluth, 2010, and chapter 10, *PET*). This constitutes a significant change in gender-based patterns of political preferences, which has potentially radical implications for politics: in the past, the gender gap between men and women, if anything, went the other way, with women typically displaying more conservative preferences than men. The close association between the switch to the left in women's political preferences, and the expansion of women's employment in service sector jobs, however, means that this new feature of the electoral landscape is unlikely to shift in the near future.

Conclusions

The service transition thus creates significant new challenges for governments in both the economic and electoral arenas. On the one hand it puts pressure on existing socio-economic models, creating new kinds of choices over policy and distributional outcomes; on the other it threatens traditional coalitions based on confluences of interest in the industrial economy, and opens up opportunities for the formation of new coalitions adapted to the dynamics of political preference formation in post-industrial labour markets.

While they face common challenges, alternative 'varieties of capitalism' have experienced the transition, and responded to it, in somewhat different ways. Liberal regimes have been reasonably successful at creating employment in private service sectors. However, this employment creation has come at a cost. It has been facilitated in part by high levels of wage inequality which simultaneously generate demand for personal and consumer services by keeping relative prices low, and increase the incentives for private investment in the higher level skills required for successful expansion in high productivity knowledge-intensive sectors. It has also relied on high levels of private sector indebtedness to fuel the expansion of consumer demand for services (as well as to finance tertiary education). The experience of these regimes during the financial crisis and subsequent recession has clearly revealed that aspects of this model are ultimately unsustainable – in particular the over-reliance on the debt fuelled expansion of domestic demand (for low end services in particular) as a mechanism for employment creation. Meanwhile evidence suggests that the partially-private model of education financing is not only associated with increasingly onerous debt burdens, but may be falling short in terms of providing the skills which expansion in more dynamic knowledge-intensive service sectors requires, hinting at the importance of public investment in education in these regimes to the development of a more sustainable service sector growth strategy. In political terms, the Liberal regimes in particular face the greatest risk of an intensification of political divisions between low and high-skilled workers, since this is where these groups are most polarised in terms of their incomes, and levels of exposure to the international economy.

The co-ordinated regimes of the central European continent, meanwhile, have kept unemployment levels low in recent decades in part because their industrial export performance has remained relatively strong, and in part because rates of labour force participation in these countries remain low (the notable exception to this profile is the Netherlands, as we discuss in the book). However, even in Germany, the industrial powerhouse, de-industrialisation is taking place, and the proportion of the working-age population currently employed in traditional sectors in Germany is not significantly greater than elsewhere. The problem for these countries is that they have been less successful at expanding employment in service sectors. High rates of wage equality have the simultaneous effects of keeping relative wages and prices for personal and consumer services high, restricting the expansion of demand and employment, and reducing the incentives for individual investment in the higher level skills which successful competition in ICT-intensive service sectors require. In the past, low rates of tertiary enrolment in these regimes were not a problem, because they were dovetailed with the highly developed apprenticeship-based vocational training systems upon which their comparative advantage in industrial sectors relied. In the current era of ICT-intensive growth, however, restricted tertiary enrolment is likely to prove more problematic. Further, the effective exclusion of large numbers of women from labour market participation in these regimes as a result of low levels of (public and private) childcare provision and restricted service sector employment opportunities, raises concerns first of all relating to equity, but also relating to the sustainability of the welfare state (as the core of the male industrial workforce shrinks in size, the affordability of welfare state provision must come into question in the absence of an expansion of service sector jobs and female employment). It is in these regimes in particular that the potential for radical change stemming from the increasing gender gap in political preferences seems greatest. As the number of working women creeps up in these countries, and with it the demand for public service provision and employment, one possible outcome could be a political shift to the left.

Finally, the social democratic co-ordinated regimes of Northern Europe have (to varying degrees) successfully combined employment creation with equality in recent decades by several means. First, the expansion of public service employment has served in some measure to compensate for restrictions on job creation in low-skilled service sectors (like personal services) in which the capacity for productivity growth is low. Second, public subsidisation of school and college based education all the way from the pre-primary through to tertiary levels has ensured high rates of tertiary enrolment, even though the wage premia available to highly educated workers are low in relative terms. Finally, as in Germany and other co-ordinated regimes, wage co-ordination itself has played an important role in ensuring the continued competitiveness of export sectors. These countries have performed well also in terms of gender equity, with female participation in labour markets facilitated through the creation of public sector jobs in services, and a range of welfare state policies such as the provision of state subsidised childcare. The future sustainability of this strategy in *economic* terms, of course, depends on its continued affordability, and, in an era of de-industrialisation, this increasingly relies on the capacity of these countries to generate expansion in high productivity, ICT-intensive service sectors. To this end, continued high levels of investment in schools and college based education, beginning at the earliest levels, will be key. Ironically, though, successful expansion in high-end services could simultaneously pose a threat to the *political* sustainability of this strategy. As increasing numbers of highly skilled workers move out of sheltered welfare sectors and into high-end service sectors which are exposed to the international economy, the challenge for governments will be to maintain cross-class coalitions supportive of high levels of public provision, equality and taxation. In this context, the large cohort of working women in Scandinavian countries (who rely on these policies to facilitate their labour force participation and employment) is likely to have an increasingly critical political role to play in anchoring these coalitions.

Anne Wren is a Research Associate of the Institute for International Integration Studies at Trinity College, Dublin, where she directed a Marie Curie Excellence Team research project on 'The Political Economy of the Service Transition', financed by the European Commission, between 2005 and 2010.

References

Ansell, B. and Gingrich, J. (2013) 'A tale of two trilemmas: varieties of higher education and the service economy', in Wren, A. (ed.) *The Political Economy of the Service Transition*, Oxford, Oxford University Press.

Autor, D. H., Levy, F. and Murnane, R. J. (2003) 'The skill content of recent technological change: an empirical exploration', *Quarterly Journal of Economics* 118 (4): 1279-1333.

Barnes, L. (2013) 'The political economy of working time and redistribution', in Wren, A. (ed.) *The Political Economy of the Service Transition*, Oxford, Oxford University Press.

Cuhne, F. and Heckman, J. J. (2007) 'The technology of skill formation', *American Economic Review* 97 (2): 31-47.

Goldin, C. D. and Katz, L. F. (2008) *The Race Between Education and Technology*, Boston, The Belknap Press of Harvard University Press.

Gregory, M., Salverda, W. and Schettkat, R. (2007) *Services and Employment: Explaining the U.S. European Gap*, Princeton, Princeton University Press.

Hall, P. and Soskice, D. (2001) *Varieties of Capitalism: The Institutional Foundations of Comparative Advantage*, Oxford, Oxford University Press.

Heckman, J. J. and Jacobs, B. (2010) 'Policies to create and destroy human capital in Europe', *NBER Working Paper* No. 15742.

Iversen, T. and Rosenbluth, F. (2010) *Women, Work, and Politics: The Political Economy of Gender Inequality*, New Haven, Yale University Press.

Iversen, T. and Soskice, D. (2013) 'A political-institutional model of real exchange rates, competitiveness, and the division of labor', in Wren, A. (ed.) *The Political Economy of the Service Transition*, Oxford, Oxford University Press.

Iversen, T. and Wren, A. (1998) 'Equality, employment, and budgetary restraint: the trilemma of the service economy', *World Politics* 50 (4): 507-74.

Meidner, R. (1974) *Co-ordination and Solidarity: An Approach to Wages Policy*, Stockholm, Bokforlaget Prisma.

Mitchell, J. (2012) 'Student debt rises by 8% as college tuitions climb', *Wall Street Journal* 31.5.2012.

Nelson, M. and Stephens, J. (2013) 'The service transition and women's employment', in Wren, A. (ed.) *The Political Economy of the Service Transition*, Oxford, Oxford University Press.

Rehm, P. and Wren, A. (2013) 'Service expansion, international exposure, and political preferences', in Wren, A. (ed.) *The Political Economy of the Service Transition*, Oxford, Oxford University Press.

Rehn, G. (1985) 'Swedish active labour market policy: retrospect and prospect', *Industrial Relations* 24 (1): 62-89.

Stigliz, J. (2012) 'Debt buries graduates' American Dream', *USA Today Weekly International Edition* 13-15.7.2012.

Wallerstein, M. (1990) 'Centralised bargaining and wage restraint', *American Journal of Political Science* 33 (4): 982-1004.

Wren, A., Fodor, M. and Theodoropoulou, S. (2013) 'The trilemma revisited: institutions, inequality, and employment creation in an era of ICT-intensive service expansion', in Wren, A. (ed.) *The Political Economy of the Service Transition*, Oxford, Oxford University Press.

Wren, A. (ed.) (2013) *The Political Economy of the Service Transition*, Oxford, Oxford University Press.

Welsh Labour in power: 'One Wales' vs. 'One Nation'?

David S. Moon

Here be dragons

As working people across Britain marched on May Day 2007, the Labour Party was in government in Wales, Scotland, London and Westminster. Five years on, only the Welsh Government remains under Labour control and, as First Minister, Carwyn Jones AM is the party's most senior elected figure. Governing alone since the 2011 Assembly elections, the minority Welsh Labour government thus finds itself tasked with demonstrating what a Labour administration stands for as a viable alternative to the harsh and economically dangerous cuts of the Conservative-led Coalition Government at Westminster. It is in this light that Ed Miliband describes the Labour government in Wales as 'charting a course' for a future Westminster government and Ed Balls declares that 'the UK can learn from what Carwyn Jones is doing in Wales' (Williamson, 2013).

Yet strangely, like ancient mariners' charts, today's maps of British politics might as well read 'here be dragons' across the Principality for all that is widely known of Welsh politics. Whilst the forthcoming Scottish referendum leads to breathless commentary from politicians and columnists, mentions of Wales mainly arise as ricochets from adversarial sniping, such as David Cameron's repeated attacks upon the Welsh NHS at PMQs, or Michael Gove's insinuations that employees should view the GCSEs of Welsh pupils as of lesser worth than those set in England. In all such cases Wales exists not in and of itself, but as a point of reference (and warning) for English concerns; even discussions over devolving tax powers to the National Assembly are reported (see Wright, 2013) in terms of how 'English people who relocate to Wales may get tax breaks' (and what of the Welsh already living in Wales one hesitates to ask?).

This entirely negative, Tory-framed image of Labour Wales is an embarrassment. In only 14 years Wales has been transformed, constitutionally, from a country without a directly elected devolved body, to one with a National Assembly wielding primary legislative powers. In this newly enhanced governmental context, the Welsh Labour government is forging its own, different path to the neo-liberalism practiced at Westminster – much as it did under Rhodri Morgan during the periods of the Blair-Brown governments. Yet, since the economic crash, the 'classic' social democratic politics practiced by Labour in Wales has found itself closer to the party's national leadership than it was – a step ahead of comrades in England even – and if Welsh Labour is indeed charting possible routes Miliband's 'One Nation' agenda might follow, then it deserves greater attention.

The constitutional is political

The purpose of this article, therefore, is to identify and present several interesting elements of Welsh Labour politics which may provide insights into the wider issues the labour movement is grappling with as it struggles to return to power at Westminster. This includes matters of social policy, ideology and rhetoric. It can only be a rough sketch and in selecting topics to discuss areas of very real significance are relegated to secondary concerns. Foremost among these is the issue of seemingly greatest interest to the Welsh Government itself, the ever changing constitutional settlement in Wales. Others have written in greater detail regarding this agenda than is possible here. Furthermore, whilst the future constitutional balance of the Union is important for all of Britain's component parts, it is arguably of less salience to the issues broached in this article. Still, a brief catch up may be in order.

From 1998 to 2011 the National Assembly for Wales had only secondary legislative powers and none regarding tax and borrowing, curtailing its ability to institute major changes. With the unlocking, via referendum, of the primary legislative powers held in the Government of Wales Act 2006, this situation has changed and in November 2012 Royal Assent was given to the first ever Bill passed by the Assembly (notably, an Official Languages Bill giving equal status to the Welsh and English languages inside the Assembly). The 'debate' over devolving additional powers never stops, however, and focuses now upon the Silk Commission and its 2012 report advocating greater financial powers and responsibilities for the Welsh Government, as well as recent calls from Jones to devolve extensive additional powers over areas such as policing and the criminal justice system (Henry, 2013). While Jones's 'wish list' appears, questionably, to have not been run past Labour's Westminster leadership first, in the context of such vocal pressure for change Miliband, Balls et al. nevertheless need to pay attention to Wales as well as Scotland, apropos the future nature of the Union. What of more immediate and transferable policies, however?

Social democratic still

With regards to policy, Labour Wales demonstrates alternative routes in a number of key areas, though not all will appeal. In education, the ill-tempered parries between Leighton Andrews AM, the Welsh Government's ever ambitious Minister for Education, and Michael Gove point to the two governments' different approaches: Welsh Labour have rejected any two-tier system in secondary examinations. Gove's back-tracking over scrapping GCSEs was a small vindication of this, yet Assembly plans to take direct control of schools away from local authorities speaks to continuing problems.

On jobs, meanwhile, recognising that leaving youth unemployment to the market in a liquidity crunch is folly, the Welsh Government have invested heavily in interventionist schemes such as Job Growth Wales, which aims to create 4,000 new jobs a year for young people and was recently praised by Ed Balls for showing the way forward on unemployment (Welsh Government, 2012). Other large scale investment includes 'Superfast Cymru', boosting the roll-out of high speed fibre broadband to 96 per cent of the population with the related aim of creating further jobs. Also hugely ambitious and symbolic is the decision to bring Cardiff Airport into public ownership after years of declining passenger numbers; as London dithers over Heathrow, the Welsh Government intends to sell the national airport as 'Terminal 6', opening up the South West for commuters and business. Devolution of borrowing powers should also liberate additional capital revenue for investment in infrastructure.

In each case Welsh Labour displays an overt recognition of the need for interventionist government to stimulate the economy with injections of public capital at the point at which private capital has dried up. In terms of debates at Westminster, however, one key policy area deserving particular attention is Labour's management of the NHS in Wales.

Caring for Bevan's baby: NHS Wales

Cameron, as noted, has repeatedly used PMQs to attack the NHS in Wales, arguing that people in the Principality are waiting longer for operations and accusing the Welsh government of cutting funding: 'That is what you get if you get Labour: no money, no reform, no good health services.' As Secretary of State for Health, Jeremy Hunt has continued this assault, batting back any criticisms of his policies of privatisation with claims Labour is cutting health in Wales. Welsh politics' low salience means that such rhetoric might well have negative ramifications for Labour's campaign to reclaim Westminster. Rather than confront the Prime Minister's jibes at PMQs, however, Miliband tries to ignore them, leaving the task of refuting Coalition attacks to the Welsh Government. Yet to find a hearing in the mainstream political narrative the latter's argument are worth airing.

First, Welsh Labour point out that, despite the findings of the Holtham Commission in July 2010 that under the Barnett formula Wales was already being underfunded by £300 million a year, the Coalition is instituting huge cuts to the Welsh budget, which at £1.8 billion over the next four years – a 42.6 per cent real terms cut in the Welsh Assembly Government's capital budget Labour claim – are deeper than those made to Scotland and Northern Ireland. It is within the context of these deep and disproportionately targeted cuts that the Welsh Government claims to have nevertheless safe-guarded NHS funding and service provision in Wales, in contrast to Coalition claims they have cut funding. The situation is naturally more complex than either side would like to admit.

The Welsh government have in fact maintained the size of the NHS budget in Wales in cash terms. Under Labour, 43 per cent of the devolved budget is invested in health and social services, the £6.3 billion funding for the NHS in Wales making up the largest single portion of the Welsh Government budget. Furthermore, as Welsh Labour emphasise, direct comparisons of figures for Wales and England are in any case inaccurate because social care is not included in the figures in England, unlike in Wales where health and social care are in the same pot. This, they claim, provides the health budget in Wales with greater protection at a time when local councils in England are cutting back social care. Nevertheless, a policy of maintaining levels of health service investment in cash terms still amounts to a real terms cut in funding. While spending per head on health services over 2010 to 2012 was higher in Wales than in England, this advantage will have eroded and indeed reversed before 2015 (see National Audit Office, 2012). Before ceding to Cameron the narrative of Welsh Labour health 'cuts' versus Coalition safeguarding, however, the Chair of the UK Statistics Authority judged in December 2012 that NHS spending in England was *also* lower in real terms after the Coalition's first two years in government than when Labour left office. Cuts to health service funding, Labour can thus truthfully point out, are far from a Welsh phenomenon.

On waiting times, the picture is also murky. This is mainly because the targets being judged are not like for like, allowing the figures to be spun in different ways. For one thing, Welsh NHS Trusts are not bound by the 18-week waiting target set in England. Wales' summary statistics instead refer to its own 26 and 36-week measures. Furthermore, there seems to be confusion when comparing when waiting lists 'start'; in Wales, they refer to the total time from referral by a GP or other medical practitioner for hospital treatment; in England, waiting times start on the day the hospital receives the referral letter, or when the first appointment is booked. So who is right? Perhaps, as the BBC concludes, 'everyone and no-one' (Davies, 2012)?

In the face of Tory attacks on the 'unreformed' Welsh health system a clearer answer is possible. From the earliest days of New Labour health 'reforms', Welsh Labour charted a different course, including setting their face against the use of the long discredited PFI mechanism in the NHS and the market derived competitive model of health service delivery adopted in England. As such, as well as having much smaller PFI obligations than other parts of the UK, Welsh Labour continues to assert their support for a publicly owned, publicly delivered health service in the face of what Jones describes as 'a health service in England that is being wrecked and privatised' (quoted in Powys, 2013). It is this classic Labour view of public sector delivery which the Tories are disparaging when they criticise a lack of 'reform'.

Yet the popular case for Welsh Labour's approach is supported by figures drawn from the National Survey for Wales in September 2012 which show 92 per cent of people satisfied with the care they received from their GP or family doctor *and* at their last appointment at an NHS hospital (Welsh Government, 2013). The Tory narrative that NHS Wales is 'unreformed' is not meant for public consumption in Wales anyway; when polled by ICM in March 2012, the Welsh rejected the suggestion that Wales should copy Andrew Lansley's infamous top-down institutional reforms to the English NHS by 4-1 (Withers, 2012). The rhetoric of 'reform' in this context is a dog-whistle for middle-England ears and Welsh Labour can easily hit back against claims regarding NHS spending by simply pointing out that, within their squeezed budget, precious health funding isn't being wasted on implementing the Coalition's deeply unpopular reforms, as it is in England.

So, does the Labour Party need to be ashamed of its stewardship of the NHS in Wales or should it, rather, learn lessons from it? There are numerous problems with health care in Wales: in a nation suffering from a particular legacy of ill health, the NHS is still recovering from a rash of ill-designed structural re-organisations under Rhodri Morgan's administrations; mental health services are poor; and current 'health reconfiguration' plans, wherein specialist services would be transferred from district general hospitals, and centralised in fewer, larger hospitals, bring very real dangers, not least in the First Minister's own constituency Bridgend, where threats posed to A&E services at the Princess of Wales hospital face considerable local anger. With regards to the Prime Minister's repeated assaults upon the Welsh Labour government at PMQs, however, while true as Cameron claims that spending is down and waiting lists up in Wales, the situation is less stark in comparison with England, *especially* when viewed alongside the tragedy which is the Health and Social Care Act 2012.

The big idea?

Nevertheless, the sceptic looking from outside might still ask, what is the 'big idea', the 'national plan' the Welsh Government offers now it has primary law making powers? Shadow Secretary of State Owen Smith MP is clear:

> our message is what it's always been: we're delivering a Labour government that's seeking to govern in the interests of working people in Wales just as we always have done, and we're looking to deliver measures which deliver as comprehensively and collectively and as equitably as we possibly can. … We are Labour. We are a Labour government in Wales, implementing Labour values and Labour policies. (Quote from author's interview with Owen Smith, December 2012)

Understated, yes, but what's not for Labour to like? Welsh Labour demonstrates that social democratic politics need not mean the sky falling in: far from perfect, it still shows alternatives exist to the neo-liberalism of the past and present. But, while devolution has often been touted for its possibilities regarding cross-border policy learning, as I have argued elsewhere (Moon, 2012), the nation-specific 'Clear Red Water' rhetoric Welsh Labour previously used to justify its policy programme has made this harder than was necessary. More than this, however, if the Welsh example is to influence the direction of the British Labour manifesto, the rhetorical and ideological basis of the party's approach is not unproblematic. What then can a 'One Nation' Labour Party learn from Welsh Labour in these regards?

'One Wales' Labour

It is worth at this stage stepping back in time to 2007. Then, having failed to win a majority of seats in that year's National Assembly election – and faced with impossibly vacillating Liberal Democrats – the Welsh Labour Assembly Group found itself in coalition talks with the nationalists, Plaid Cymru. These resulted in a document entitled 'One Wales', setting out the basis for a red-green coalition. This included: a commitment, without qualification, to a referendum on further powers for the Assembly at or before the 2011 Welsh elections; a Convention looking at the case for further powers leading up to the referendum; an independent commission to review the Barnett formula through which Wales was allocated funding; and a commitment to consider devolving powers to Wales over criminal justice; and a new Welsh Language Act.

While supporters of the deal, especially in the party leadership, described it as one which would 'deliver 100 per cent of Labour's manifesto' (Rhodri Morgan, in Davie, 2007) and 'about parties of similar ideas working together' (Edwina Hart AM, in Osmond, 2007, 33), more than any other recent political event – including the 1997 devolution referendum – there was a great deal of anger and opposition to the proposal across the party. The deal was thus attacked publicly for providing 'an Assembly vehicle' to transport 'the separatists and cultural and political nationalists' to 'the gates of independence' (Kim Howells MP, in Osmond, 2007, 8) whilst ignoring the 'lack of any binding common philosophy between the two parties' and taking away 'the focus … from the real social justice issues that the people of Wales clearly want us to concern ourselves with over the next four years' (Karen Sinclair AM, Ann Jones AM and Irene James AM, in BBC News, 2007).

Behind closed doors at the special party conference called to discuss and vote on the deal, the arguments of opponents were fiercer still (1). One North Walian CLP delegate described Plaid as a 'racist' party, telling members that it was 'not alright to negotiate with a party because only part of it [i.e. the part in North Wales] seems racist'. A different delegate warned Southern comrades that 'in North Wales, English speakers are second class citizens' warning of 'Wales becoming a greater Gwyneth'. Speaking to both cheers and laughter one MP loudly declared the agreement to be 'a Trotskyist plot' which amounted to 'transitional demands' aimed at delivering a nationalist agenda. A Women's Forum member called upon delegates to 'vote for your socialist principles, not for nation-alist ones'.

Altogether, roughly three quarters of those who spoke at the conference did so in opposition to 'One Wales', with views split across all layers of the party. The result of the conference vote itself, however, was a resounding victory for supporters of the document, with a clear majority of both affiliates (96 per cent) and constituencies (61 per cent) voting for the deal, which passed with 78 per cent of the collated vote (notably there was no 'block' for MPs' and AMs' votes). This result had ultimately been a done deal before the special conference even opened. With the unions and delegate votes already decided albeit not formally declared, members attended and spoke already aware that 'One Wales' would be agreed. What the party sanctioned platform offered, really, was the opportunity for opponents to vent – and as shown above, vent they did.

It is important to understand the depth of feeling which surrounded Labour entering into the 'One Wales' coalition because the argument surrounding this existential decision arguably marked the recent high point of an intra-party antagonism which has historically ebbed and flowed within the Labour Party in Wales. In vulgar terms, this antagonism amounts to what has been labelled at different times as a clash between 'nationalist' and 'unionist' tendencies (Morgan & Mungham, 2000) or 'British' and 'Welsh' tendencies (Shipton, 2007). Lazily equated by some with divergent 'devolutionist' and 'devo-sceptic' opinions (see for example Davies & Williams, 2009), this is a more fluid but no less significant distinction between – to draw upon Huw T. Edwards – those who 'see the Labour Party through Welsh eyes' and those 'seeing Wales through Labour Party eyes' (quoted in Ward, 2011, 70). In the debate today over 'One Nation' politics this is a significant division.

Arguably, moments of deep tension between these intra-party tendencies are anomalies (see Smith, 2012c); antagonisms have fizzled and crackled in the background, but only really burst to the surface once or twice: in the 1950s between Aneurin Bevan and those such as Megan Lloyd George and Cledwyn Hughes arguing for a Parliament for Wales; and in the great schism at the tail end of the 1970s where the charismatic opposition of Neil Kinnock, Leo Abse et al. trampled all over Michael Foot's devolution plans. In these cases constitutional reform was intimately linked to questions of identity, with fears on both sides that change or stasis would irrevocably damage their preferred self-conceptions of the party and Wales – be that Welsh 'culturalist' or internationalist 'Labourist', say.

If nationalism in Wales was of a civic variety (as it is in Scotland), rather than cultural and linguistic (as it actually is), undoubtedly fewer within the labour movement would fear its influence. Yet, to a large extent such concerns have abated with devolution, as its gradual deepening and the accrual of further powers has passed by with only minimal grumbling around questions of 'Welshness'. Even fears at the 'Cymricisation' of Wales' civic space linked to an increasing emphasis on the promotion of and spending on the Welsh language – which the latest census shows is nevertheless in decline – has raised less than the odd yelp, even now as the Welsh Government debates enforcing new legal standards over the use of Cymraeg by public and private bodies. The abject failure of True Wales, the leading body arguing against further devolution of powers, to gain any traction – despite being in many regards a classic 'old Labour' Unionist grouping (albeit with Tory backing) – is emblematic of this.

The proposition embedded in 'One Wales' – of formally breaking bread with the hated nationalists – was thus the first and so far last truly seismic eruption of the aforementioned ideological rift post-devolution. What it ultimately signified was a general recognition of Welsh Labour's evolution since 1998 into a particular type of soft-nationalist party (in the Assembly Group, at least). Welsh Labour went to war internally over 'One Wales', but following the cathartic moment offered by the special conference and subsequent 'Yes' vote, the conflict deflated once again, a victor, long since dominant, confirmed. Even before the titular coalition document, Welsh Labour was espousing what might be called a 'One Wales' identity politics, in so doing operating within a post-devolution 'Welshminster Consensus' around Cardiff Bay – largely forged by itself – within which the major parties, even to an extent the Tory Group, operate.

The 'Welshminster consensus'

This Welshminster Consensus embodies: (i) soft-nationalist cultural politics and political rhetoric; (ii) devo-maximising constitutional reform; and (iii) a social democratic policy agenda. Amongst other things this consensus is the outcome of day-to-day working in a political community which is small and close. With only 60 AMs in Cardiff Bay – compared to 650 MPs at Westminster – the atmosphere is familiar and relaxed; first names are used in the Senedd chamber; and cross-party socialising amongst AMs, their staff, media, academics, lobbyists and civil servants in the Bay's local pubs is regular and the norm. This more 'intimate' setting has been helped by an electoral system which makes coalition government and minority deals the rule; the Assembly was designed from the start to foster a politics which broke from the adversarial 'Westminster model'.

That a Welsh nationalist viewpoint would exert a stronger influence upon the Labour Assembly Group than the Welsh Parliamentary Labour Party was thus in a sense to be an inevitable corollary of devolution; after all, whilst in Westminster the handful of nationalists are easily dismissed and ignored as 'kooks and crazies' by 'big three' parliamentarians, until 2011 Plaid Cymru AMs constituted the second largest group in the Assembly and from 2007 to 2011 were Labour's coalition partners there. From within this cultural milieu, and recognising a general growth in Welsh identity amongst the population, Welsh Labour's rhetoric has trumpeted the national particularity of a 'small nation' and people with 'Welsh values' and 'Welsh attitudes' which are very different to 'the English way' and thus make necessary specific 'Made in Wales' policy solutions to match (see Moon, 2012).

Its tanks placed firmly on the political ground its 'One Wales' coalition partner once controlled, Welsh Labour has sedimented its position as the ideological hegemon of post-devolution politics: every element in 'One Wales' which caused critics to denounce it as a nationalist Trojan horse – the focus on Barnett, powers and promoting *Cymraeg* – are now owned by Welsh Labour: they are basic points of Carwyn Jones' political philosophy. The result, as Plaid Cymru leader Leanne Wood described, is a broadly soft-nationalist consensus:

> the Welsh nationalist agenda has progressed quite significantly since the setting up of devolution. What we've seen happening in Wales is that the British parties, the unionist parties, have taken on a lot of the policies that we've been advocating. We advocated the reform of the Barnett formula, measures to defend the Welsh language, for example, and the parties have come on board, on to our territory. There's no differ-ence between the parties on those issues. And the same goes for extending devolution, in terms of the referendum that we won last year. All parties are united around progressing that agenda. (Quoted in Sparrow, 2012)

This is the Welshminster Consensus within which a 'One Wales' Labour Party operates but also controls; and against Wood's claims, it has arguably spiked Plaid's guns: all of this is the legacy of one-party dominance in Wales – or 'Labourland' as it has been called in the past.

Where critics within Welsh Labour saw 'One Wales' as a route to Plaid's advancement, the actual legacy has been Plaid's decline to third party status – overtaken by the Conservatives – and the increasing relevance of the titular question of Syd Morgan and Alan Sandry's insightful article (2011): 'What is Plaid Cymru for?' What Morgan and Sandry fear is that, just as Labour have become more culturally nationalist, so Plaid have been 'gradually slipping into a UK devolutionary, Cardiff Bay, but *Labour-led* consensus'. After all, if there are two social democratic, soft-nationalist parties in Wales, doesn't one become surplus to requirements? Looking from across the border, what Ed Miliband might see in Wales is an example of a party which has managed to articulate an electorally successful social democratic politics via appeals to national solidarity and culture. In the current search for a 'One Nation Labour' politics, the appeal is clear.

'One Nation Labour' in Wales?

But a 'One Wales' political approach is symptomatic of a problem for Labour: how do you have 'One Nation' politics in a nation of nations like the UK? More than any other, Owen Smith has sought to square this seeming circle, addressing it across a number of intelligent articles. Indeed, the term 'One Nation' was deployed by Smith (2012a) in the *New Statesman* even before Miliband's 2012 Conference speech, wherein he argued that:

> Welsh Labour's success is both a product of the left and radical traditions of Wales and of a renewed sense of national mission. It is this fusion of progressive politics with national mission – this nation-building from the left – that Labour needs to understand and adopt across the UK.

Writing for the *Western Mail*, Smith (2012b) described how, yes, 'modern Britain is a nation of nations, with traditions and culture, heritage and history, accents, dialects and even languages that divide us' but argues that 'there are as many things, more important things perhaps, that bind us together, that also make us One Nation' as '[c]ommon values, cherished institutions and unifying experience … form a shared, British identity which is tolerant and inclusive, and embraced by the majority of people who live in these isles.' A 'One Nation' politics would thus entail '[a]n approach that respects devolution and the distinctions which it reflects and responds to, but which also recognises the greater strength of our people when we pull together; across classes and countries, faiths and nations.' Though Smith does not address it directly, the question of whom Labour's 'people' are is the absolute key to the 'One Nation' debate at *all* national levels.

'The people as the rest of us'

This is currently confused: on the one hand, there is talk of communities, treated as groups in the classic pluralist sense; on the other, party figures including the leader have invoked notions of not only British patriotism, but also English national identity meant to sit alongside Welsh and Scottish. However, defining 'One Nation' upon boundaries of national identity and nationalist identifiers is hazardous: Ed Miliband has already been accused of insensitivity in his call for mandatory English proficiency for public workers for his total failure to take on board the realities of Welsh language communities, especially in North West Wales (Henry, 2012). If the UK is a 'nation of nations' the danger is that the Labour Party/parties in Cardiff Bay and Westminster will appeal to different national 'levels' of this multi-layered construct.

The answer is to cleave, again, to socialist roots. If 'One Nation' politics are to mean something beyond the vague or the regressive, they have to be a call not to divisions between 'national people(s)' – be they 'Welsh people', 'English people' or 'British people' – but rather to the 'people of the nation' – that is, to 'the people of Wales', 'the people of England', 'the people of Britain' or – yes – even 'the people of Europe'. The first articulation of the 'people' appeals to a demarcated grouping in which *all* those situated within the national space are included – rich or poor, banker or jobseeker – with inside/outside divides mapped onto national borders, even where, as in the case of the UK, these split apart greater transcending peoples. Where appeals are made, however, to the second articulation of 'the people', the entity being referred to is not to everyone as a whole or a unity – *all* the Welsh, or *all* the British – but to that set of people left-wing thinker Jodi Dean calls 'the people as the *rest of us*': i.e. 'those of us whose work, lives, and futures are expropriated, monetised, and speculated on for the financial enjoyment of the few' (Dean, 2012, 69).

It is upon the shoulders of this 'proletarianised' figure – the 99 per cent, so to speak – which crosses national borders rather than obstinately resting upon them, that a One Nation Labour politics can find its feet in our nation of nations. This is the ideology which underpins such declarations as Ed Miliband's, made at the 2012 Conference, that: 'I don't believe that solidarity stops at the border. I care as much about a young person unemployed in Motherwell as I do about a young person unemployed here in Manchester' (Miliband, 2012). Embracing the 'people as the rest of us' reminds us that, whilst social democratic politics is our goal and a post-devolution Britain our playing field, the purpose of Labour is not to swallow, trumpet or fulfil nationalist agendas as Leanne Wood would have us think. As an active, interventionist government, Labour in Wales provides lessons the British party should attend to. The lesson from Wales is also, however, that even if it may win votes, political rhetoric which frames policies and ideology in nationalistic terms must be rejected, not embraced. The people of Labour's 'One Nation' are inter-nationalist at all national levels: they are both *inter*national and inter*national*. The populist message for the party to take is therefore simple: working people of the nation(s) unite as one!

David S. Moon is Lecturer in Politics at Liverpool University.

References

BBC News (2007) 'Opposition to Plaid deal spreads', *BBC News* 4.7.2007, at
    http://news.bbc.co.uk/1/hi/wales/6268230.stm.
Davie, E. (2007) 'Coalition means "suicide" for Labour', *PoliticsHome* 5.7.2007, at
    http://centrallobby.politicshome.com/latestnews/article-detail/newsarticle/coalition-means-
    suicide-for-labour/.
Davies, D. (2012) 'Governments in a spin over NHS hospital waiting times', *BBC News* 9.2.2012,
    at http://www.bbc.co.uk/news/uk-wales-politics-16962001.
Davies, N. and Williams, D. (2009) *Clear Red Water: Welsh Devolution and Socialist Politics*,
    London, Francis Boutle.
Dean, J. (2012) *The Communist Horizon*, London, Verso.
Henry, G. (2012) 'Ed Miliband accused of "insensitivity" to Welsh language', *Western Mail*
    15.12.2012.
Henry, G. (2013) 'Policing should be Wales' own responsibility, says Carwyn Jones', *Western
    Mail* 18.2.2013.
Miliband, E. (2012) speech to Labour Party Annual Conference, 2.10.2012, at
    http://www.labour.org.uk/ed-miliband-speech-conf-2012.
Moon, D. S. (2012) 'Rhetoric and policy learning: on Rhodri Morgan's "Clear Red Water" and
    "made in Wales" health policies', *Public Policy and Administration*, early view available at
    http://ppa.sagepub.com/content/early/2012/08/22/0952076712455821.abstract?rss=1.
Morgan K. and Mungham, G. (2000) *Redesigning Democracy: The Making of the Welsh
    Assembly*, Bridgend, Seren.

Morgan, S. and Sandry, A. (2011) 'What is Plaid Cymru for?', *Clickonwales: The IWA News Analysis Magazine* 11.5.2011, at http://www.clickonwales.org/2011/05/what-is-plaid-cymru-for.

National Audit Office (2012) *Healthcare Across the UK: A Comparison of the NHS in England, Scotland, Wales and Northern Ireland,* London, National Audit Office.

Osmond, J. (2007) *Crossing the Rubicon: Coalition Politics Welsh Style*, Cardiff, Institute of Welsh Affairs.

Powys, B. (2013) 'Over-rule on the cards at health?' *BBC News* 27.2.2013, at http://www.bbc.co.uk/news/uk-wales-politics-21607060.

Shipton, M. (2007) 'Lib-Lab pact on way amid fear of Plaid win in 2011', *Western Mail* 9.5.2007.

Smith, O. (2012a) 'Why Labour needs the nation', *New Statesman* 28.9.2012.

Smith, O. (2012b) 'Labour's One Nation respects the proud and distinct parts of the UK', *Western Mail* 23.10.2012.

Smith, O. (2012c) Tudor Watkins Memorial Lecture, 2.11.2012, at http://www.owensmithmp.co.uk/smith-delivers-inaugural-tudor-watkins-memorial-lecture/.

Sparrow, A. (2012) 'Plaid Cymru leader: we can only prosper if we do things for ourselves', *Guardian* 12.9.2012.

Ward, P. (2011) *Huw T. Edwards: British Labour and Welsh Socialism*, Cardiff, University of Wales Press.

Welsh Government (2012) 'Jobs growth Wales', 18.5.2012, at http://wales.gov.uk/topics/educationandskills/skillsandtraining/jobsgrowthwales/?lang=en.

Welsh Government (2013) 'National Survey for Wales, January to March 2012: Health results', 29.1.2013, at http://wales.gov.uk/topics/statistics/headlines/compendia2009/national-survey-wales-jan-mar-2012-health/?lang=en.

Williamson, D. (2013) 'Ed Balls: the UK can learn from what Carwyn is doing in Wales', *Western Mail* 8.2.2013.

Withers, M. (2012) 'Polls show "only 7 per cent" of people in Wales want independence', *Western Mail* 1.3.2012.

Wright, O. (2013) 'English people who relocate to Wales may get tax breaks', *Independent* 24.2.2013.

Note

1. These notes are based upon personal transcription of speeches at the event by the author.

Reviews

An emergent consensus on public services

The Relational State

Edited by Graeme Cooke and Rick Muir

IPPR, 2012

Reviewed by Catherine Needham

At the launch of the national evaluation of the Personal Health Budgets pilots in early 2013, the evaluation team expressed some surprise about how much people had valued the time spent sitting down with a professional to talk at length about their interests and needs – rather than this being merely the means to an end of a care plan and a budget (for the full evaluation report see Forder et al., 2012). Such a finding will not surprise contributors to this new IPPR collection on *The Relational State*. Although the editors make a claim for the novelty of the content – stating that it replaces the 'virtual silence across much of the centre-left on questions relating to public services and statecraft' (p. 3) – it is best seen as a culmination of work on public services emanating from a range of bodies. These include the IPPR itself, Demos, the Young Foundation, NESTA, the New Economics Foundation, Participle and the RSA. Together these works signal an emergent consensus on the value of relational accounts of public services: that 'recognising the importance of human relationships could revolutionise the role of the state', as the subtitle of the collection puts it.

The lead essays in the collection are provided by Geoff Mulgan and Marc Stears; they each provide a wide-ranging and provocative piece, followed by shorter articles on specific aspects of public services which situate them in the context of Mulgan's account of the 'relational state'. The editors are keen to highlight that there are key differences in what is argued by different contributors: this is not a single blueprint for action. Mulgan, for example, takes a much more instrumental view of relationships and a more interventionist view of the state than Stears. Mulgan, along with the editors and contributors such as Nick Pearce, seem to be explicitly looking for a new 'centre-left statecraft' for Labour, and to make peace with its governing legacy along the way. The editors position the 'relational state' argument as a 'blend of "Blue Labour" and "New Labour" thinking' (p. 10). Others such as Stears are less haunted by the 'dominant statecraft of the last Labour government' (p. 8) and more concerned about the democratic potential of a more relational politics. Whereas for Mulgan better relationships are a crucial element of achieving better outcomes in public services, in Stears' essay democratic relationships have intrinsic value. States themselves cannot be relational, Stears argues; they can only protect the time, the places and the institutions that enable people to engage in relational activity. He frames the state as an 'agent of standardisation', whereas 'nothing is more flexible, contingent, ever-changing, particular or beyond control than a proper, rewarding, human relationship' (pp. 38-9).

The editors (Graeme Cook and Rick Muir) provide a substantive introductory discussion of these themes and tensions (which is a useful entry point for readers in a hurry). The whole collection is thoughtful and challenging, and it is impossible to do justice here to its full range of ideas and proposals. There are four areas, though, where I would have liked to see the authors set out their ideas more fully.

The first is how people working in public services can be supported to acquire the skills required by the relational state. Mulgan argues that the skills and capabilities of people working in a relational state will be different to those in the 'delivery state': 'the ability to empathise, communicate, listen and mobilise coalitions of citizens and professionals to achieve social goals' (p. 10). For example, he suggests that we 'make healthcare more like education, deliberately aiming to raise the skills of the public through, for instance, courses or e-tutorials' to support people with diabetes and dementia. Such findings resonate with those of the University of Birmingham Policy Commission (2011) into the future of local public services, which identified new roles that staff will play in twenty-first century public services – 'navigators', 'brokers', 'storytellers', 'resource-weavers' – as part of a process of supporting citizens to be 'co-authors of their own lives' (1).

Supporting professionals in acquiring these skills and building effective relationships is a key challenge, but one which professional bodies, universities and service providers are not yet well set up to meet. There needs to be an emphasis on how to share learning across professional silos and to ensure that those engaged in relational services, such as health care assistants, social care workers, and classroom assistants, are not excluded from a process which is explicitly targeted at the 'professions'. To embed the right attitudes from workers, the editors suggest that 'a bargain could be struck' in which professionals are freed from 'the worst aspects of a distracting compliance culture' and rewarded for excellence ('with their own performance rigorously held to account') (p. 18). Mulgan calls for professionals to be appraised through 360-degree feedback from key stakeholders. Yet there is a clear danger that such performance measures become part of the 'audit culture' which Stears identifies as being completely antithetical to the relational revolution. Alex Heitmuller's contribution on the NHS raised some concerns for me here. He makes the point that the NHS is starting to appreciate the importance of relational aspects of care, 'but lacks a consistent approach' (p. 53). However, the idea of a consistent approach across the whole NHS seems entirely against the spirit of relational public services.

A second area where more development would be useful is on how the emphasis on relationships will intersect with an outcomes-focus. Mulgan writes: 'Some of the goals of government have to be concerned with outcomes – fewer families in crisis, for instance, or better survival rates in hospitals. But others should be relational...' (p. 25). But events at Mid-Staffordshire remind us that the link between outcomes and relationships of care is a crucial but complex one, and that neglect of the relational can end up also compromising the 'harder', more measurable outcomes.

These complex links between relationships, outcomes and culture are underplayed in the book, and would merit further attention, particularly in the context of the Francis Report. A recent article about the NHS argues that over-worked nurses make their working lives manageable by identifying some patients as 'poppets' and lavishing care on them, whereas others are treated merely as 'parcels' to be processed (Maben et al., 2012). Rustin's (2005) work on why social workers reacted the way they did in the case of Victoria Climbie described the social workers' responses as a form of 'mindlessness' in the face of unfathomable suffering. Such cases, extreme though they are, remind us of the difficulties of sustaining relationships in understaffed, demoralised, stigmatised services. Such ethical issues are not limited to the traditionally caring professions. In *Impossible Jobs in Public Management* (1990), Hargrove and Glidewell write of the difficulty of acting ethically in large, complex state bureaucracies in which staff have limited legitimacy, high conflict and low professional authority, and include inner-city teachers and police officers in the scope of their argument.

Third, I would have liked more discussion of how the contributors' enthusiasm for devolving funding down to the individual level through personal budgets and pupil premiums will intersect with the emphasis on relationships. The literature on social work has highlighted potential tensions between individualised funding and a therapeutic social work based on valuing relationships. Houston uses Alex Honneth's critique of individualisation in modern society to argue against personalisation: 'at the heart of [personalisation] is an impoverished ontology, namely one that fails to accord sufficient weight to the primordial and existential realities of human inter-dependence, inter-being and symbolic interaction. This is not to deny the importance of choice and control in life planning ... but rather to argue that they are best positioned within an ontological framework where inter-being, sociality and the socially constructed nature of the self are to the fore' (Houston, 2010, 842).

Fourth, more attention to broader issues of political economy in the relational state is needed, a critique indeed which Nick Pearce makes of Mulgan in the book. A suggestion by the editors that 'the level of funding can be weighted to favour those with less power or resources of their own (as is the case with the pupil premium)' (p. 13), suggests a very unambitious approach to the redistribution of wealth. Hilary Cottam's point that 'the most important tool for finding a job is not a CV or a personal worker, but a social network' (p. 50) sets out a necessary but not sufficient criteria for finding a job in a shrinking economy in which jobs are scarce. Optimism about the role of civil society in providing public services seems somewhat naive given the disastrous impact that the government funding cuts have had, particularly on small charities.

There are some other issues which are underdeveloped in the text. The role that trade unions might play in a relational state is ignored. One contributor writes: 'Teachers need a proper, independent association to develop their professional skills and protect excellence' (p. 58), without considering that this might be a role played by trade unions. The contributors assume that much of the work of the 'relational state' will be undertaken by third sector bodies, who are not hampered by the 'compliance culture' of the state or the profit motivation of the private sector (although the NHS is included in the list of non-state bodies which seems rather disingenuous (p. 18)). These heroic claims for the third sector have been made for a decade whilst the evidence base around third sector contributions – and their appetite for and capacity to provide a 'supply revolution' (p. 18) – remains somewhat uncertain. Axel Heitmuller's claim that we should look to the experience of payment-by-results in welfare to work for ideas on how to reform health is an odd reading of the welfare to work evidence base. A couple of the other contributors call for more local elections along the lines of the Police and Crime Commissioners without dwelling on the legitimacy problems that such elections are likely to generate on the basis of low turnouts. However, these are minor gripes in a book which is stimulating and ambitious, and whose ideas will be central to the future of public services.

Catherine Needham is Senior Lecturer in Public Policy and Public Management at the Health Services Management Centre, University of Birmingham.

References

Forder, J. et al. (2012) *Evaluation of the Personal Health Budget Pilot Programme*, London, Department of Health.

Hargrove, E. and Glidewell, J. (1990) *Impossible Jobs in Public Management*, Lawrence, University of Kansas Press.

Houston, S. (2010) 'Beyond homo economicus: recognition, self-realisation and social work', *British Journal of Social Work* 40 (3): 841–57.

Maben, J., Adams, M., Peccei, R., Murrells, T. & Robert, G. (2012) 'Poppets and parcels: the links between staff experience of work and acutely ill older peoples' experience of hospital care', *International Journal of Older People Nursing* 7 (2): 83-94.

Rustin, M. (2005) 'Conceptual analysis of critical moments in the life of Victoria Climbie', *Child and Family Social Work* 10 (1): 11–19.

University of Birmingham Policy Commission (2011) *When Tomorrow Comes: The Future of Local Public Services*, Birmingham, University of Birmingham.

Note

1. The Public Services Academy at Birmingham University is beginning a programme of work around the theme of the Twenty-First Century Public Servant, looking at how to provide training and support for the workforce in the development of these skills.

How did the Conservatives change?

The Conservatives Since 1945: The Drivers of Party Change

Tim Bale

OXFORD UNIVERSITY PRESS, 2012

Reviewed by Robert Saunders

How do parties change? It is almost a truism that parties stand or fall on their capacity for reinvention, and politicians now routinely campaign on platforms of 'hope' and 'change'. For much of the twentieth century, the supreme practitioner of political adaptation was the British Conservative Party. Ted Heath memorably promised to 'change the course and the history of this nation', while Margaret Thatcher vowed to 'change the heart and soul' of the people. Running for the leadership in 2007, David Cameron urged his supporters to 'change to win'. To be electable, he warned, the party must 'change its language, change its approach, start with a blank sheet of paper'.

Yet the nature, scope and drivers of party change remain under-theorised, an insight that forms the basis of Tim Bale's new book. As in his previous study, *The Conservative Party From Thatcher to Cameron*, Bale operates in the terrain between history and politics, testing models drawn from political science against thickly descriptive historical examples. This refreshingly interdisciplinary approach has established him as one of the leading scholars of modern Conservatism, whose work can be read with profit by general readers and scholars from both disciplines.

Bookended by the landslide defeats of 1945 and 1997, each chapter covers a single period of government or opposition (1945-51; 1951-64; 1964-70; 1970-74; 1974-79; 1979-97). For each case-study, Bale assesses the extent of change in three areas: the public face of the party; its internal organisation; and the policies it sought to enact. These are tested against three main 'drivers' of change: election defeat; the role of the leader; and the existence of a 'dominant faction'; supplemented by such 'additional drivers' as think tanks, interest groups or the pressure of events.

The first of his indicators proved most resistant to change. Candidates, MPs and ministers remained largely white, male and middle class, drawn disproportionately from Oxford, Cambridge and the public schools. Constituency parties proved deaf to the charms of working class and ethnic minority candidates, in the belief that 'working-class candidates' were 'inadequate in … campaigns and often of doubtful use in parliament'. Safe seats, in particular, 'expect to be represented by people of distinction' (pp. 89-90). Leaders rarely involved themselves in such matters, even when they were from atypical backgrounds themselves. Thatcher was notoriously indifferent to the prospects of Tory women, while John Major did little to promote candidates in his own, non-university image.

The party machine received more sustained attention, though it was not always the Rolls Royce operation its opponents believed. At its best, it was a formidable campaigning and fundraising machine: in 1950, for example, it secured up to 90 per cent of postal votes for the Conservatives, securing eleven seats from Labour and denying Attlee the majority that might have carried him through a full parliamentary term. Skilful fundraising allowed the party to outspend Labour at every national election until 1994, paying for publicity, market research and field operations on a scale beyond Labour's wildest dreams. In the 'pre-campaign' before the 1959 election, the Conservatives exceeded Labour's publicity budget by more than four to one, and in the summer of that year it was briefly the biggest advertiser in the UK. By the 1970 election – a contest Labour had been widely expected to win – the Conservatives were employing nearly three times as many agents as Labour on double the salaries.

Yet few leaders showed much interest in party organisation, meaning that improvements 'were rarely institutionalised, even when they were seen to be successful' (p. 91). Churchill did not set foot in Central Office in his fifteen years as party leader, while Macmillan failed to recognise in 1960 the General Director he had appointed three years earlier. Cecil Parkinson, who became Party Chairman in 1981, later confessed that he had struggled to find the party's offices on his first day at work. The results were rather haphazard. An internal report described the party's election broadcasts in 1964 as 'makeshift, ramshackle and absolute agony' (p. 116), while the campaign in February 1974 was a shambles. The Campaign Guide was sent out as a bundle of photocopied sheets, unbound and without an index; other literature arrived late or not at all, while phone calls went unanswered and unreturned.

The leadership was much more engaged in policy change, though it was not always the most authoritative leaders who did most to drive reform. Churchill, 'a man for whom … almost anyone would have done almost anything', was 'an absentee king' who spent more time on his memoirs than on the business of opposition (p. 304). Thatcher, by contrast, emerges as the most dynamic driver of policy change, but the biggest shifts came in the early years of opposition when her leadership was most vulnerable.

Bale plays down the role of think tanks and pressure groups, as well as the influence of 'business' or 'the City'. Though the Conservatives undoubtedly saw themselves as the party of business, they had little faith in the policy prescriptions of its representatives. Thatcher did not meet with the CBI for nine months after becoming leader, and was frustrated by its enthusiasm for incomes policy and 'the whole corporatist paraphernalia' (p. 240). Nor did backbenchers or party workers exert more than marginal influence. Heath expressed a common view among the leadership, telling a backbencher that there were 'three sorts of people in this party: shits, bloody shits and fucking shits' (p. 165).

Such comments reinforce the perception of a 'magic circle' directing operations from above. Yet Bale finds 'dominant factions' to be neither as common nor as cohesive as is widely believed. Indeed, the clearest example of such a group emerges as John Major's team. 'Built not so much on ideology but on the shared conviction that the Tories had no realistic alternative but to keep calm and carry on, this group ran the party until it crashed to defeat in 1997' (pp. 285-6).

Fortunately for Major, such factions neither needed nor always benefited from the presence of a charismatic leader. The so-called 'Thatcherites', for example, were always less cohesive than popular myth suggested, and Thatcher's abrasive style acted as an increasingly centrifugal force. After 1945, as in later periods, 'Those who helped put their party back on track … were an often amorphous bunch of people who were by no means always in complete agreement – the better known among them spending as much time jostling for position or in profitable employment as they did remaking conservatism or the Conservative Party' (pp. 46-7).

What conclusions can be drawn from all this? Bale does not propose a unifying model for party change; on the contrary, his account is consciously eclectic and multicausal. In this respect, it offers a valuable debunking of the extravagant claims made in more schematic studies. He rightly insists on the interdependence of his variables, in an 'inter-play of ideas, interests, institutions, and individuals' (p. 317). Nor is this the only strength of Bale's book. The chapter on 1974 to 1979 makes a substantial contribution to the literature on Thatcherism, showing how much policy work was done in opposition, how early the decisive changes took place, and how much of this was signalled to the public in opposi-tion. The treatment of Northern Ireland is also a strength, not least in its refusal to isolate the subject from the normal process of policy. Bale pays full attention to the Conservatives' determination to engage in a battle of ideas with the left, and he is particularly good on the changing instruments through which these ideas were communicated to the public. He writes well on new media and the use of market research, especially the shift in the Thatcher era from targeting 'opinion formers' (like clergy, teachers and doctors) to a direct appeal to 'ordinary' people through tabloid newspapers and the middle-brow media.

Change was not, of course, always beneficent; nor was it always directed from within. One of the most striking phenomena of this period was the collapse of party membership, from a nominal muster roll of 2,805,032 members in 1953. This included a dynamic student movement and a vibrant Young Conservative wing; yet the story thereafter was of contin-uous decline, reaching catastrophic proportions in Scotland, Wales and the great cities. It would be interesting to know what Bale sees as driving this change, not least because of its salience to the first of his three indicators. For if the image of the party at Westminster altered little over this period, the face it presented in the constituencies became consider-ably greyer and more wrinkled. In the early 50s, one might go to the Conservative Club in the hope of picking up a husband; by the 1980s, one was more likely to be picking up one's granny.

This was part of a wider transformation, which eroded two pillars of previous Conservative success: its claim to represent the *nation*, rather than any single class within it; and its ability to tap into a network of social organisations that were not explicitly partisan. The shift from a national, ostensibly classless alliance that stood, in some sense, above 'party politics', to a professional outfit rooted in the South of England marked a major party change. Its drivers are still only dimly understood, though they were reflected in the party's own language. Churchill's manifesto in 1945 had not even mentioned the word 'Conservative', and the Scottish party campaigned as 'Unionists' until the mid-1960s. It was not until 1948 that candidates for borough elections routinely fought as 'Conservatives', rather than as 'ratepayers' or 'municipal' candidates. In this respect, the period after 1945 marked a 'coming out' process for a politics that dared not speak its name. That shift was as important to the rebranding of Conservatism as any number of new logos; and in its consequences, it was almost certainly more costly.

Robert Saunders is a Lecturer in History at Oxford University. He is the co-editor of *Making Thatcher's Britain* (Cambridge University Press, 2012).

Back issues

RENEWAL 19.1 spring 2011

Editorial Leading Labour *Robin Archer* **Changing fortunes of social democracy** Spain: phoenix turned to ashes *Paul Kennedy* France: the frozen pendulum *Ben Clift* Italy: post-social democracy *Davide Vampa* Scandinavia: discursive smoke screens *Mikko Kuisma* Ireland: a new opportunity *Jean O'Mahony* Latin America: social democracy reborn? *Rick Muir* **Essay** Beyond the Westminster model *Patrick Diamond* **Commentary** The power of union-community coalitions *Amanda Tattersall* Marketising higher education: American lessons *Bob Samuels* **Review** Nicholas Phillipson *reviewed by James Stafford*

RENEWAL 19.2 summer 2011

Editorial The long game *Ben Jackson and Martin McIvor* **Features** Rediscovering Labour's soul *Josh Booth and Will Brett* Making sense of Maurice Glasman *Alan Finlayson* Re-embedding the housing market *Matt Griffith* Comprehensives and social mobility *Vikki Boliver and Adam Swift* Localism and the left *Phil Parvin* **Commentary** The 'forward march' of Scottish nationalism *Gerry Hassan* The plot against the NHS *Colin Leys and Stewart Player* **Notebook** Community organising in Germany *Leo Penta* **Reviews** Eric Hobsbawm *reviewed by David Leopold* Steve Richards *reviewed by Hopi Sen*

RENEWAL 19.3/4 autumn 2011

Editorial We need to talk about Gordon *Hopi Sen* **Building a better capitalism** A different economy for Britain *John Denham* The entrepreneurial state *Mariana Mazzucato* The short-lived return of Keynes *Roger Backhouse and Bradley Bateman* **Interview** Long live neo-liberalism? *Colin Crouch interviewed by Dan Leighton* **Where is the opposition?** Building a movement against the cuts *Adam Ramsay* Opposing the age of austerity *Gregor Gall* Transforming Labour *Gavin Hayes* Punch and Judy politics *Richard Toye* What Ed Miliband can learn from Thatcher *Robert Saunders* **Commentary** Democracy, collective action, and the state *Marc Stears and Tim Horton* Blue Labour and the limits of social democracy *Ed Rooksby* **Essays** Retrieving the public sphere *Robert Tinker* Renewing the case for electoral reform *Jacqui Briggs* **Reviews** Will Straw et al. *reviewed by Noel Thompson* Marian Barnes *reviewed by Catherine Needham* Catherine Needham *reviewed by David Rowland* David Marquand *reviewed by Andy Tarrant* Nicholas Shaxson *reviewed by Matthew Richmond*

RENEWAL 20.1 spring 2012

Editorial Alex Salmond's journey *Ben Jackson* **Taking on the 'predators'** The lessons of neo-liberalism *Daniel Stedman Jones* Philosophical foundations for 'good' capitalism *Martin O'Neill and Thad Williamson* Fending off locusts by shouting *Ed Turner* Political strategy for a new economy *Graeme Cooke* **Interview** What they don't tell you about capitalism *Ha-Joon Chang interviewed by James Stafford* **Essay** The UK's economic performance under Labour *Dan Corry, Anna Valero and John Van Reenan* **Notebook** The other Israel *Toby Greene, Alan Johnson and Noam Leshem* **Review essay** Civic republicanism in Zapatero's Spain *Stuart White* **Reviews** R. Daniel Kelemen *reviewed by Andy Tarrant* Alistair Darling *reviewed by Robert Saunders*

RENEWAL 20.2/3 autumn 2012

Editorial Twenty years of *Renewal Ben Jackson* **Labour's opportunity** The identity crisis of Jon Cruddas *Sunder Katwala* Lessons from the Conservatives *Tim Bale* My Labour, New Labour, twenty-first century Labour *Phil Wilson* **Interview** Obama and American progressivism *an interview with Robert Kuttner* **The return of the common good** The republic, old and new *Philip Pettit* The moral economy of Occupy Wall Street *Frances Fox Piven* Who or what is to blame? *Neal Lawson* Anti-politics and what the left can do about it *William Brett* **Decentralising the left** Dilemmas of American federalism *Conor Gaffney* Rebalancing the regions *Lewis Goodall* The political economy of Scottish independence *Michael Keating* **Farewell to *homo economicus*?** Crowding effects on intrinsic motivation *Bruno Frey* The failure of executive incentive schemes *Tom Powdrill* Adam Smith and motivation crowding out *Lisa Herzog* Behaviour and the welfare state *John Welshman* **Notebook** Explaining Hollande's victory *Jocelyn Evans* **Reviews** Ferdinand Mount *reviewed by Danny Dorling* Richard Bourke and Alvin Jackson *reviewed by James Stafford* Diane Coyle *reviewed by Bill Blackwater* Jan-Werner Müller *reviewed by Christopher Brooke* Stephen Brooke *reviewed by Olivia Bailey* Martin O'Neill and Thad Williamson *reviewed by Natan Doron*

RENEWAL 20.4 winter 2012

Editorial One Nation Labour and Sweden's 'people's home' *Katrine Kielos* **For a more radical social democracy** The radical potential of democratising capital *Joe Guinan* On the death of financialised capitalism *Bill Blackwater* **The strange victory of German conservatism** The state of German conservatism *Clara Maier* German ordo-liberalism and the politics of vitality *Werner Bonefeld* **Essays** 'Common schools for a common culture' *Diane Reay* How France leapfrogged the UK in women's representation *Rainbow Murray* **Roundtable** What's left of the left? Social democrats in challenging times *Mark Wickham-Jones, Richard Toye, Ben Clift, Magnus Feldmann, John Kelly, James Cronin* **Review essay** Histories of debt *James Stafford* **Reviews** Andrew Adonis *reviewed by Sally Tomlinson* John Denham et al. *reviewed by David Coates*

Back issues cost £9.99 (individuals) and £30 (institutions) each plus post and packing (£2 UK, £4 overseas)

RENEWAL

Become a subscriber…

Subscription rates are (for four issues):

Individual subscriptions
£27.50

Institutional subscriptions
£110

PDF-only subscriptions
£12.50

Please send me one year's subscription, starting with Issue No. _____

I enclose payment of £_____

Name _____

Address _____

_____

_____ Postcode _____

Please return this form (a copy will do) with a cheque or money order made payable to Renewal. Send to: Renewal, c/o Lawrence & Wishart, 99a Wallis Road, London E9 5LN.

Payments can be made online using all credit or debit cards (except American Express). Please visit www.lwbooks.co.uk for details.

Back issues cost £9.99 (individuals) and £30 (institutions) each plus post and packing (£2 UK, £4 overseas).